# The Greatest British Olympians

First published by Carlton Books Limited 2011


Carlton Books Limited
20 Mortimer Street
London W1T 3JW



A CIP catalogue record for this book is available from the British Library.
10 9 8 7 6 5 4 3 2 1

ISBN: 978-1-84732-812-0

Printed in China

Senior Editor: Conor Kilgallon
Project Art Editor: Luke Griffin
Design: Brian Flynn
Picture Research: Paul Langan
Production: Maria Petalidou

FSC
www.fsc.org
MIX
Paper from responsible sources
FSC® C101537

TEAM GB

# The Greatest British Olympians

## A celebration of Team GB's outstanding athletes, past and present

Neil Wilson

Foreword by
**Sir Chris Hoy, MBE**

CARLTON

# Contents

Introduction ..... 6
Foreword ..... 8

**Athletics:** Harold Abrahams / Chris Brasher ..... 10
Lord Burghley ..... 12
Sebastian Coe ..... 14
*Chariots of Fire* – The Real Story ..... 16
Lynn Davies ..... 18
Jonathan Edwards ..... 20
Sally Gunnell ..... 22
David Hemery ..... 24
Albert Hill ..... 28
Kelly Holmes ..... 30
Denise Lewis ..... 34
The Coe vs Ovett Era ..... 36
Eric Liddell / Douglas Lowe ..... 38
Steve Ovett ..... 40
Ann Packer / Mary Peters ..... 42
Mary Rand ..... 44
Tessa Sanderson ..... 46
Daley Thompson ..... 48
Allan Wells ..... 52
The Olympic Walkover ..... 54
**Boxing:** Chris Finnegan / Harry Mallin ..... 56
Dick McTaggart / Terry Spinks ..... 58
**Canoeing:** Tim Brabants ..... 60
**Cycling:** Chris Boardman ..... 62
Nicole Cooke ..... 64
Chris Hoy ..... 66
Victoria Pendleton / Jason Queally ..... 70

Rebecca Romero ... 72
Bradley Wiggins ... 74
**The London 1908 Games** ... 76
**Equestrian:** Derek Allhusen / Henry 'Harry' Llewellyn ... 78
Richard Meade ... 80
**Fencing**: Gillian Sheen ... 82
**Hockey:** Sean Kerly ... 83
**Modern Pentathlon:** Stephanie 'Steph' Cook / Jim Fox ... 84
**Rowing:** Jack Beresford ... 86
Matthew Pinsent ... 88
Steve Redgrave ... 90
**Sailing:** Ben Ainslie ... 94
Rodney Pattisson ... 98
Iain Percy ... 100
Shirley Robertson and Sarah Ayton ... 102
**Shooting:** Malcolm Cooper ... 104
**Britain's Football Hat-trick** ... 106
**Swimming:** Rebecca Adlington ... 108
Duncan Goodhew / Judy Grinham ... 110
Anita Lonsbrough / Adrian Moorhouse ... 112
Paul Radmilovic / Henry Taylor ... 114
David Wilkie ... 116
**Tennis:** Charlotte Cooper ... 118
**Weightlifting:** Launceston Elliot ... 119
**The Austerity Olympics 1948** ... 120
**The Changing Face of the London Olympic Games** ... 122

Index ... 124
Picture Credits ... 128

# Introduction

**Britain's record at the Olympic Games is exemplary. In the history of Olympic competition, few nations have produced such a consistent roster of famous names.**

Together, they have won 209 gold medals, up to the end of Beijing 2008. A Briton has won gold in at least one event at all 26 Games (gold medals were not originally awarded), a record unequalled among more than 200 nations expected to participate in the Games of the XXX Olympiad at London 2012.

All of those winners were sporting giants of their own age. Some, from the more recent Games, are sporting giants. Steve Redgrave, the winner of five gold medals in Rowing, Chris Hoy, who won three golds in a single Games in Track Cycling, and Kelly Holmes, double Olympic champion at 800m and 1500m in Athletics, need no introduction. The feats of others, such as Launceston Elliot, who was Britain's first Olympic medal winner in 1896, and Charlotte Cooper, the the first woman to win an individual Olympic event, are lost in the mists – and myths – of time.

Yet when the Games open at the new Olympic Stadium in east London on 27 July 2012 and London becomes the first city to host a third Games, all will deserve their place in the great pantheon of Britain's Olympic past. This book tells the stories of 58 individual champions in 14 sports, among the 26 that will be contested in 2012. As with all selections, the list is subject to debate, but what no one can dispute is that those who fill the ranks of sporting heroes in this book were the pick of their many generations.

Baron Pierre de Coubertin, the visionary who brought the ancient Games of Olympia back to life in 1896, chose to embrace the philosophy of his time that the most important thing is not to win but to take part, just as the most important thing in life is not the triumph but the struggle. True as that is, it is those to whom triumph belongs that we remember. It is to those who wore the red, white and blue badge of Great Britain that this book celebrates.

Mark Foster leads Team GB at the Opening Ceremony of the Beijing 2008 Olympic Games – his fifth Games.

# Foreword

**The Olympic Games is unrivalled as the greatest spectacle in the sporting world. The Games attracts billions of viewers worldwide who are enthralled by more than 10,000 Olympic athletes battling it out for glory across 26 sports.**

British athletes have always shone on this incredible stage, with gold-medal-winning performances that stretch back to the birth of the modern Olympic Games, when Launceston Elliot won Weightlifting gold at the Athens 1896 Games.

Since then, our athletes have continued to excel across a broad spectrum of sports from Athletics, Swimming and Cycling to Sailing, Rowing and Equestrian, as well as many more. Who could forget the amazing achievements of Daley Thompson as he competed against the great Jürgen Hingsen to claim two successive Decathlon golds in the 1980s? Or the astonishing Rowing performances of Sir Steve Redgrave and Sir Matthew Pinsent as they won nine gold medals between them in what became a virtual dynasty spanning six Olympic Games? Also now the stuff of legends are the Athletics duels between Sebastian Coe and Steve Ovett at 800m and 1500m that saw world records tumble almost on a weekly basis and gold medals shared between them at Moscow 1980 and Los Angeles 1984.

There's plenty to admire among the modern crop of athletes too, all of whom now have their place in the history books. Rebecca Adlington in Swimming, Ben Ainslie in Sailing and Kelly Holmes in Athletics are among the long list of British athletes who have become household names, not just in the UK but right across the world.

All of these athletes' achievements have filled me with admiration. Tales of amazing performances, glorious wins, stunning new records, podium places and dramatic comebacks have entertained me and inspired me during my own career. Contained on these pages are the stories of athletes I've watched and heard about all my life – some of them are also now my contemporaries in Team GB.

To stand on the podium and have a gold medal hung around your neck is the stuff of dreams. The British team is sure to shine at London 2012 when those gold-medal dreams will hopefully be turned into reality. I hope you enjoy reading about the accomplishments of this exceptional group of men and women in the history of the Olympic Games and the incredible journey that British athletes have taken, before the next chapter begins at London 2012.

**Sir Chris Hoy, MBE**

BRITAIN
BEIJING 2008

# HAROLD **ABRAHAMS**

**Born:** 15 December 1899, Bedford, England
**Height:** 1.84m (6ft)
**Weight:** 80kg (176lb)
**Olympic highlights:**
1920: 100 and 200m quarter-finals
1924: 100m gold, equal OR; 4 x 100m Relay silver; 200m 6th

**Harold Abrahams was to be the last Briton to win the Olympic 100m gold medal for 56 years when he won in Paris in 1924. Certainly he was the first – and probably the last – to write to a national newspaper to ask for himself to be dropped from an Olympic event.**

Abrahams, the youngest son of Jewish-Lithuanian immigrants, competed relatively unsuccessfully at 100m and 200m in the 1920 Olympic Games at the age of 20 but it was when he came under the tutelage of a legendary coach, Sam Mussabini in the winter before the next Games that he showed his full potential.

Mussabini taught him to be very exact and extremely professional in his sprinting and training. One idea was to run a precise number of strides of an exact length in 100m. Abrahams laid pieces of paper in training runs to the exact stride measurement and tried to spear each on his spiked shoes.

Abrahams dips at the finish of the 100m at the Paris 1924 Games. He didn't need to worry – the clock showed he had won the race by one-fifth of a second, a huge margin.

In 1924 he set an English record for Long Jump of 7.38m – it was to survive 32 years – and won the 100m and Long Jump at the AAA Championships. He was then chosen for 100m, 200m, the Long Jump and the 4 x 100m Relay team at the Games.

Abrahams thought it was too much and would lessen his chances. He thought it improper to complain personally, so wrote to the *Daily Express* anonymously criticising the selection. Officials took note and deselected him.

He was not favourite to win the 100m but in the quarter-finals and semi-finals Abrahams ran personal bests, each time tying the Olympic record at 10.6 seconds, and began to believe he might win. He described the night before the race as feeling 'like a condemned man feels just before going to the scaffold'. But Mussabini's final words of advice were: 'Only think of two things – the report of the pistol and the tape. When you hear one, just run like hell till you break the other.'

Abrahams did. He gradually opened a small gap in the final 50m and won by 61cm, again equalling the Olympic record (although electronic clocks showed he actually ran faster at 10.52 seconds).

At that time, medals were sent by post. Abrahams's gold arrived with insufficient postage paid and he needed to pay to receive it.

He also finished sixth in the 200m, and helped the British Relay team to a silver medal in the 4 x 100m Relay in a time which was to stand as a national record for 20 years. He retired the following summer after damaging a thigh muscle.

**'Only think of two things – the report of the pistol and the tape. When you hear one, just run like hell till you break the other.'**

**Sam Mussabini**, Abraham's coach, advises him before the 100m final in 1924.

# CHRIS **BRASHER**

**Winning the gold medal in the 3000m Steeplechase at the Melbourne 1956 Games at the age of 28 was far from the most noticeable achievement in the extraordinary life of Chris Brasher. It was not even the first time one of his feats had been immortalised.**

**Born:** 21 August 1928, Georgetown, Guyana
**Olympic highlights:**
**1952:** 3000m Steeplechase final
**1956:** 3000m Steeplechase gold, OR

Brasher (no. 26, centre) clears the water jump during his gold-medal run in the 3000m Steeplechase at the Melbourne 1956 Games.

## 'I squeezed out what little talent I possessed.'

Brasher began as a 5000m runner at university, winning at the World Student Games in 1951, but his first serious claim to fame was as one of two pacemakers for Roger Bannister when he ran the mile in under four minutes in 1954. It is ironic that while Bannister and the other hare, Chris Chataway set world records, only Brasher won Olympic gold.

It was unexpected. The oil company executive was Britain's third choice behind 1952 bronze medallist John Disley and Eric Shirley and, although all three made it to the final, Brasher was the least fancied. But 300m from the finish, at the fourth-from-last barrier, Brasher elbowed his way between Norwegian Ernest Larsen and Hungarian Sándor Rozsnyói to win in an Olympic record time.

Almost immediately his win was thrown into doubt. Rozsnyói was given the win because Brasher was judged to have impeded Larsen. The British team appealed – surprisingly, supported by the three men who finished behind Brasher. After three hours of deliberation the appeal was upheld and Britain had won its first gold in an individual event for 20 years.

Brasher's life in the public spotlight was only just beginning. He retired from the track and the oil industry to become sports editor of the *Observer* newspaper, before becoming a regular face on British television as a reporter for the *Tonight* current affairs programme. In 1969 BBC Television appointed him as Head of General Features. He stayed for three years before going into business with former rival Disley. Together they made their fortune before, in 1979, they attended the New York Marathon after hearing tales from members of their athletic club.

So entranced with the concept of a mass marathon were they that on their return, Brasher wrote an article in the *Observer* entitled 'The World's Most Human Race'. It began with the words: 'To believe this story you must believe that the human race can be one joyous family...' He ended it by asking whether London might stage such a race.

The *Observer*'s editor brought Brasher and Disley together with the relevant authorities at a lunch and from that was born, in April 1981, an event that has become as traditional in the capital each year as the Lord Mayor's Show. By the time Brasher died, in 2003, the race had been run by more than half a million people and was to become the world's largest single annual charity fund-raising event.

# LORD **BURGHLEY**

**Born:** 9 February 1905, Stamford, England
**Height:** 1.8m (5ft 11in)
**Weight:** 70kg (154lb)
**Olympic highlights:**
1924: 110m Hurdles 1st round
1928: 400m Hurdles gold OR
1932: 4 x 400m Relay silver; 400m Hurdles 4th; 110m Hurdles 5th

**Lord Burghley (full name David George Brownlow Cecil) was the outstanding British all-round hurdler between the two world wars, and something of a character. His feats were immortalised under the fictitious name of Lord Andrew Lindsay in the Oscar-winning film *Chariots of Fire*.**

Burghley, heir to the 5th Marquis of Exeter, was born at Burghley House – the family's 16th-century country house – and was a direct descendant of the great Robert Cecil, Elizabeth I's Chief Secretary of State. Educated at Eton, he competed at the Paris 1924 Games at the end of his freshman year at Cambridge, a year, oddly, when he had failed to win a Blue for Athletics. He was eliminated in the first round of the 110m Hurdles. It was three years later, in 1927, that he first found popular fame among his contemporaries.

That year, his last at Cambridge, he became only the second man ever to run around the Great Court of Trinity College in the time it took its clock to strike twelve, and the first to do it since the clock's striking time had been reduced by five seconds years earlier. It became the basis for a classic scene in *Chariots of Fire*, but the role instead was given to another Olympic champion, Harold Abrahams. It was because of the licence taken that Burghley refused to allow his name to be used, and refused to see the finished film when it was released in 1981, six months before his death.

The year 1927 was also when he set his only world record, 54.2 seconds in the 440 yards Hurdles, in the successful defence of an AAA title he had won for the first time a year earlier. The record did not survive even the day in which it was set because an American was to break it in Nebraska. Burghley won eight titles at AAA Championships and became the president of the Amateur Athletic Association, a function in which he took such great pride that he obtained the number plate AAA1 for his Rolls-Royce.

Burghley was the first hurdler known to have practised his technique by setting matchboxes on the top of barriers and attempting to knock each off without disturbing the hurdle. It honed a skill that saw him become the British record holder in all three hurdling events – the 120 yards, 220 yards and 440 yards – the 220-yards time lasting as a record for 23 years.

Burghley won Olympic gold in Amsterdam in 1928, running an Olympic record time of 53.4 seconds, which beat the defending champion and world-record holder Morgan Taylor (USA), who finished third. In 1930, at the first Empire Games, he won gold medals for England in the 400m Hurdles and in the

Lord Burghley (no. 444, centre) powers away from USA's Frank Cuhel (far right) to win gold in the 400m Hurdles at the Amsterdam 1928 Olympics.

4 x 400m Relay, and two years later, was chosen as Britain's Olympic team captain at the Los Angeles 1932 Games. He ran the fastest time of his career of 52.2 seconds in the 400m Hurdles, but was to finish fourth, beaten to the bronze medal by Morgan Taylor by a fifth of a second. Consolation came in the form of a second Olympic medal, a silver, as a member of the 4 x 400m Relay team, when the British quartet ran a European record time.

By this time he was already the Conservative Member of Parliament for Peterborough. He had to ask Parliament for leave of absence to attend the Los Angeles 1932 Games, which required lengthy return journeys by ship and train. He held the seat until, in 1943, he was appointed war-time Governor of Bermuda. He was later to be mayor of his home town of Stamford.

At the age of 28, immediately after his retirement from competition, he was elected a member of the International Olympic Committee, a position he retained for 48 years. He did not lose his athleticism. Invited on the RMS *Queen Mary* during her sea trials in the Irish Sea in 1936, he ran a lap of the promenade deck wearing evening dress, approximately 400 yards, in a hand-timed 57 seconds. He also remained active on dry land, keeping his own pack of hounds at Burghley House and hunting into later life, even after an arthritic hip forced him to use a stick for walking. He never lost his connection with his first love, athletics. He was president of the British Amateur Athletic Board for 40 years and president of the International Amateur Athletics Federation, which governed the sport globally, for 30 years.

For the London 1948 Games, Burghley, a leading advocate of London's right to host, was chosen as chairman of its organising committee. He delivered a Games that at current prices cost only £77 million, and which made a modest profit. 'The great test was taken; and the organisation rose gloriously to the supreme challenge,' wrote IOC president J. Sigfrid Elstrom in the official report.

# SEBASTIAN **COE**

**Born:** 29 September 1956, London, England
**Height:** 1.75m (5ft 9in)
**Weight:** 54kg (119lb)
**Olympic highlights:**
1980: 1500m gold; 800m silver
1984: 1500m gold; 800m silver

**Sebastian Coe was the most prolific world-record breaker ever to come out of Britain and the only man to defend the Olympic 1500m title successfully. In an international career often interrupted by illness he set nine world records outdoors, and three indoors, and won 10 major championship medals.**

Coe was born in London but grew up in Yorkshire, where his father, Peter, an engineer in the Sheffield steel industry, realised his eldest son's talent for running and set out to acquire the knowledge to coach him. 'There is nothing revolutionary about what I did for Seb but it was tailor-made for his physique,' said Coe senior.

Coe was a winner from the earliest days, at school sports, at county cross-country races and in club races. At 16 he was national youth 1500m champion and English national school champion at 3000m.

Coe's desperate desire to retain the 1500m title he won at Moscow 1980 is written on his face as he crosses the line in triumph at the Los Angeles 1984 Games.

By 1976 he was improving his times at 1500m and one-mile distances in almost every race, but he was far from the best in Britain. He was seventh in the Olympic selection race in 1976 and only fourth in the AAA Championships and his father decided that he should move down a distance to 800m.

His intention was to improve his son's speed for the longer event, but in 1977 Coe made his breakthrough as a two-lap runner. He won the national indoor title and the European Indoor Championship in a championship record time before finally that year setting a new British 800m record of 1:44.95.

It was 1979 when the Coe phenomenon took off. In the space of 41 days, he broke three world records: the 800m in a time of 1:42.33 and the mile in 3:48.95, both in Oslo, and finally the 1500m in 3:32.03 in Zurich.

He warmed up for Olympic year by breaking the world 1000m record in 2:13.40, so for a brief time held four world records, before compatriot Steve Ovett broke his mile record by a fifth of a second 30 minutes later.

So when the British team arrived in Moscow as one of those nations not boycotting the 1980 Games, the rivalry of the two Britons was the story. Most felt Coe could not lose the 800m but that Ovett could win the 1500m. Coe himself admitted he held that view. The reverse happened.

Coe did not run his best 800m. 'I chose this day of all days to run the worst race of my life. I suppose I must have compounded more cardinal sins of middle-distance running in one and a half minutes than I've done in a lifetime,' said Coe at his post-race press conference. He finished up with the silver medal.

He had a second chance in the 1500m six days later and took it, avoiding all the tactical mistakes of the previous race and beating Ovett into third place. The ecstatic smile of relief on Coe's face as he crossed the finishing line made a historic photograph. 'I sank onto my knees, it was such a marvellous relief,' he said.

In 1981 Coe went to Florence in Italy and broke the world 800m record in 1:41.73, and then to Oslo and improved his own world 1000m record to 2:12.18. Then in nine days in August he broke the one-mile record twice, running 3:48.53 in Zurich and 3:47.33 in Brussels. In his last three mile races, he had broken the record each time.

His competitive season in 1982 was interrupted by another stress fracture, and he was beaten into second place at 800m in the European Championships and withdrew from the1500m. He then withdrew from the year's Commonwealth Games and in 1983 pulled out of the World Championships when unwell in hospital for treatment.

In the 1984 Olympic trials, he was beaten at 1500m, but winning the silver medal in the 800m at the Los Angeles 1984 Games brought him to the peak he needed, as he went on to defend his 1500m title.

Proof that he was still the best came when he accelerated down the straight, winning by six metres in an Olympic record of 3:32.53. As he crossed the line, his anger at those who had written him off exploded and he pointed angrily. '"Who says I'm finished?"' was my first thought. It was anger bordering on hatred. It is not something I am proud of,' he wrote years later.

More satisfaction came two years after when, finally, he won a major title at 800m at the European Championships, but he was never again to run in the Olympic Games. In the trials for Seoul 1988, he managed only fifth place.

Such was the public outcry at the thought Coe would be unable to defend his title that Juan Antonio Samaranch, the president of the IOC and a friend, invited him to compete as his personal selection, a wild-card. However, public opinion caused Samaranch to change his mind and the invitation was withdrawn.

**'I consider him one of the finest athletes we have ever seen. He set not just new records but new standards in the way he ran.'**

**Andreas Brugger**, promoter of the Weltklasse meeting in Zurich.

Right: Coe was chosen to carry the British flag at the Closing Ceremony in Los Angeles 1984 after winning his two medals in the Games.

# *Chariots of Fire* – The Real Story

**The Oscar-winning *Chariots of Fire* is the movie that restored the fame of two British Olympic athletes of the 1920s. It won four Oscars and seven Academy nominations. But how much of it was a truthful reflection of the events of the time?**

Eric Liddell crosses the line to win the 400m. Also due to compete in the 100m, Liddell, a committed Christian, refused to race as the heats were held on a Sunday.

'I believe God made me for a purpose, but he also made me fast. And when I run, I feel His pleasure.' *Actor Ian Charleson speaking as **Eric Liddell** in* Chariots of Fire.

*Chariots of Fire* is certainly the most realistic movie about athletics ever produced, not least because the cast spent three months before filming being trained by a British Olympic coach, Tom McNab. They looked like runners, ran like runners and did not need extras to portray them.

The film tells the story of two men at the Paris 1924 Olympic Games – Harold Abrahams and Eric Liddell – both of them sprinters and both gold medallists. That much is true, and their story was dramatic in itself.

Abrahams, a Jewish undergraduate at Cambridge, employed a private professional coach, Sam Mussabini, a concept frowned upon by the strict amateur ethos of the age. Liddell, the son of missionary parents, refused to bid for selection for the 100m at the Olympic Games because the heats of the event would be run on the Sabbath.

It was a perfect vehicle for producer David Puttnam, who had been looking for a story about a man with a conscience and came across it while reading a historical reference book when house-bound with flu. He asked actor Colin Welland to produce a script.

Welland recognised the drama of the scenario. He was so determined to keep to its foundations that they sought the agreement of those still alive to use their actual names. All but one of the Olympic finalists in the 100m allowed their names to appear – only bronze medallist Arthur Porritt, by then Lord Porritt, declined.

He even sought the permission of Jackson Scholz to attribute to him an inspirational Bible quotation actually handed to Liddell before his race by an American team masseur. 'If it makes me look good, fine with me,' Scholz is alleged to have replied.

But where Welland felt it necessary to part company from reality was in the relationship of the two Britons. For dramatic effect and to connect them, he needed Abraham and Liddell to be rivals: a Jew motivated by anti-Semitism to go the extra mile to succeed pitted against a Christian with a conscience who was the very definition of the Victorian amateur.

In truth, Abrahams never ran against Liddell in the 100m, the event Abrahams won in Paris. And far from disapproving of Abrahams's use of a professional coach, it was Liddell who introduced the two men.

Welland's screenplay has Liddell discovering that the 100m would be on the Sabbath as the British team embarked at Dover on the cross-Channel ferry for France. Instead he takes a place in the 400m left vacant by the voluntary withdrawal of teammate Lord Lindsay.

In reality the timetable had been known for six months. The British Olympic Association and the Prince of Wales, its patron, had both made overtures to Liddell to change his mind, and the story had made headlines well in advance of the Games.

Liddell had sufficient notice of the timetable to train instead that year for the 400m and, after his win in the year's AAA championships, he travelled to Paris as one of the favourites to win.

The character represented by the fictional Lindsay was David Burghley, who indeed was an aristocrat and did practise clean hurdling by putting champagne glasses on them. But it was not the 400m and the 400m Hurdles for which he was selected in 1924, but the 110m Hurdles. It was in 1928 that he was to win gold in the 400m Hurdles.

The film also shows Abrahams running around the perimeter of the Great Court at Trinity College, Cambridge, in the time it takes the college clock to chime 12 times. In fact, Burghley was the only man in the 20th century to do it.

Welland also reversed the order of the sprints in Paris, pretending that the 200m – which Scholz won, Liddell came third and Abrahams last – preceded the 100m, where the Briton beat the American.

There were other minor fabrications. Abrahams did marry an opera singer, as the film portrays, but they were not courting while he trained for the Games. They did not meet until 1935. And Abrahams's great motivation to succeed came not from the anti-Semitism he faced, but his desire to emulate an elder brother who had competed at the Stockholm 1912 Olympic Games.

None of Welland's pretences were detrimental to the film. Only the most pedantic of observers made anything of them because the majority of movie-goers agreed that his script made a great film.

Certainly Hollywood did. Welland won an Oscar that year for the best screenplay, and the film won the Oscar for best picture. The British Film Institute selected it as the 19th most important in its Top 100 British films.

Certainly it brought renewed fame to Abrahams and Liddell, 57 years after their triumphs. Neither lived long enough to see it, while Burghley refused to allow his name to be used and declined to view the film.

Harold Abrahams rests between events during the Paris 1924 Games. Abrahams won gold in the 100m.

# LYNN **DAVIES**

**Born:** 20 May 1942, Nantymoel, Wales
**Height:** 1.83m (6ft)
**Weight:** 72.5kg (159lb)
**Olympic highlights:**
1964: Long Jump gold; 4 x 100m Relay final; 100m 1st round
1968: Long Jump 9th
1972: Long Jump preliminaries

**Lynn Davies was the first Welshman to win an Olympic gold medal in an individual event, the first winner in a field event born in Britain and the first athlete to hold Olympic, Commonwealth and European titles at the same time.**

Davies was good enough at football as a teenager to be offered terms by Cardiff City FC but, inspired by spectating at the 1958 Commonwealth Games in Cardiff, he chose athletics while training to be a schoolteacher. Triple Jump was his first event and his first Long Jump of 6.45m, into the pit at Ogmore Grammar School, where he was a pupil in Bridgend, came only four years before his Olympic success.

Davies owed his success to the 1961 appointment as Welsh national coach of Ron Pickering. He had never coached but had innovative ideas about weight training improving performance, and was also an outstanding motivator. Once, when Davies said a weight he had to lift was too heavy, Pickering lifted it himself to prove it possible. He admitted later that he had chest pains for three days afterwards.

Pickering's programme for Davies was relentless. In winter, he would be lifting up to five tonnes in a single session. He would do three sets of four squats with 227 kilograms on his back, three times his own bodyweight. 'My coach made me what I am in three and a half years of hard work,' said Davies after his Olympic victory.

Within two years of their partnership, Davies competed at both Commonwealth Games and European Championships. He was just two centimetres off the European silver medal when he finished fourth with a personal best jump of 7.72m. His breakthrough, and the stimulus that persuaded Davies to increase his workload by 30 per cent in the winter before the Olympic Games, came in Volgograd in the former Soviet Union in an international match for Great Britain. Davies lost, but only by three centimetres to world-record holder Igor Ter-Ovanesyan, who would become a friend.

He was not among the favourites at the Tokyo 1964 Games. Both Ter-Ovanesyan and the American Ralph Boston, the defending champion, had jumped beyond 8.20m. Davies had yet to achieve eight metres. Indeed, he barely scraped into the final, only managing it with his last jump of the qualifying round. 'If anyone had told me then that I would win the gold medal I would have laughed at them,' he said at the winner's press conference.

What favoured the Welshman was the weather – cold, windy and wet, common conditions in Wales. 'The Welsh gods must have been looking down on Tokyo that day. I am convinced I would not have won had it been warm and sunny,' he said.

Davies was in third place until the fifth round. Boston had told him to watch the stadium flags to judge the wind and when Davies saw them drop, he began his run. He landed at 8.07m, a phenomenal jump off a soggy cinder runway and into a slight headwind. Boston came over to tell him nobody would better it on a day like that, but with the last jump of the competition Boston came to within four centimetres. 'Watching it was agony. I was looking through my fingers,' said Davies.

When Davies returned home, he was paraded in a limousine through the streets of his small village and neighbouring Bridgend, where packs of children ran beside the car. At the millennium almost three decades later, in a country where rugby union is the national sport, his jump was voted the greatest moment in Welsh sporting history. He became known affectionately as Lynn the Leap.

Davies was to break the Commonwealth record many times. In 1966 he won the Commonwealth and European gold medals, achieving a unique hat-trick of titles. He also won the European Indoor Championship and in 1968 jumped 8.23m, which remained a British record for almost 34 years.

He was not, though, to win at the Mexico City 1968 Games. It was another gloomy day, but the competition was ended by a single jump, the American Bob Beamon's first. He landed at 8.90m, the first ever jump of 29 feet, the first even beyond 28 feet. 'I can't go on. What is the point? We'll all look silly,' Davies said to Boston. Then he turned to Beamon and said: 'You have destroyed the event.' It was a mark not beaten for more than 20 years, and was voted the athletic feat of the century. Davies finished ninth.

Davies continued to be successful, winning silver medals at the European Championships and European Indoor Championships in 1969, and successfully defending his Commonwealth title in 1970. But at his final Olympic Games at Munich in 1972, he was injured and did not qualify for the final. He retired, having improved the British record by two feet during his career, and having jumped more than eight metres in 22 separate competitions.

He went on to become a teacher, but in 1973 became director of coaching in Canada for four years, and later had a long career in Welsh broadcasting. He is president of UK Athletics.

Opposite: 'Lynn the Leap', as the Welsh called Lynn Davies, reaches out into the pit in Tokyo, where he won Long Jump gold in 1964.

**‘The Welsh gods must have been looking down on Tokyo that day.’**

**Davies,** on his 1964 Games experience.

# JONATHAN **EDWARDS**

**Born:** 10 May 1966, London, England
**Height:** 1.81m (5ft 11in)
**Weight:** 70kg (154lb)
**Olympic highlights:**
1988: Triple Jump 23rd, DNQ final
1992: Triple Jump 35th, DNQ final
1996: Triple Jump silver
2000: Triple Jump gold

**One of the greatest triple jumpers of all time, Edwards did not win Olympic gold until his fourth Games. Success came late in his career in every way. He was 29 before he won any major international championships, by which time he had been competing for 14 years, and been a British international for seven years.**

The son of a clergyman, Edwards grew up in Devon and first tried the hop, step and jump at school. He won the Devon Schools Championships, the English national Schools Championships and, when studying physics at Durham, the British universities championships. But his first competition for Britain was at the age of 22 at the Seoul 1988 Games. He was selected despite refusing to compete in the trials because his event fell on a Sunday, a day on which he had chosen never to compete for religious reasons, and he hardly justified that selection when he finished 23rd.

His first international medal came at the 1990 Commonwealth Games, when he won silver – missing the gold by just two centimetres – but a year later he declined to go to the World Championships because his event fell on a Sunday again. The Barcelona 1992 Olympic Games brought him no consolation. He failed to qualify for the final, finishing 35th of 47 competitors, and a month later was last in the Grand Prix final.

Curiously, he was selected as Britain's triple jumper at the World Cup in Havana, where he won with his final jump. A year later he won bronze at the

**'Here I was after everything that's happened and I was champion. It was almost too much. I was choking back tears.'**

**Edwards,** after winning gold at Sydney 2000.

Edwards wins the first Olympic medal of his career at Atlanta 1996, but it is a silver, not a gold, for the Triple Jump world-record holder.

World Championships, but at the 1994 European Championships he was sixth, and missed out on gold again at the Commonwealth Games that year, blood tests later showing he was suffering from a glandular infection.

Going into 1995, when he was past his 29th birthday, there was no indication that the year would be special for him. Because of the virus, he had trained lightly that winter, but he began to work on a new technique with a different coach based on one used by an American, Mike Conley. The result was apparent in his first competition of the summer. He set a new British record of 17.58m, 14cm further than his previous best.

That summer was to be the most memorable in the history of the event. In Lille, France, he won a world-class competition, which gave him confidence when he returned there for Britain in the European Cup a week later. His first jump landed at 17.90m but was not a record because of wind assistance. His next landed at 18.43m, the furthest ever achieved, and another at 18.39m, both ruled out because of excessive wind assistance. He also jumped a legal 17.72m, a new British record.

Finally, he achieved the world record in Salamanca, Spain, with a legal jump of 17.98m, an improvement by one centimetre on the oldest field-event record. He was the first British man to break a jumps world record since C.B. Fry in 1893. Even that was nothing to what followed at the World Championships in Gothenburg, Sweden, in August. His first jump landed at 18.16m, again a world record; his second at 18.29m, the first time any man had exceeded 60 feet. He was to surpass 18m once more that season, but never again.

He was elected World Athlete of the Year and the BBC Sports Personality of the Year, and had won all 14 competitions he entered. But he spent the next winter worried about repeating his success, over-analysing the reasons for success. He admitted in his autobiography: 'I know now that I created a monster in my mind.'

At the Atlanta Games, in the summer of 1996, he was the shortest-odds favourite of all, coming off a streak of 22 wins with the four longest jumps in history, but finished second to American Kenny Harrison, who had jumped only three times in the previous 16 months because of injuries.

He was second again in the 1997 World Championships, third at the 1999 World Championships and arrived at the Sydney 2000 Games, at the age of 34, having the best mark of the year of 17.62m. He entered the Games as favourite again, but the focus was not upon him that night. The world was watching Australian Cathy Freeman win the 400m and, almost anonymously, Edwards won his Olympic gold with his year's best of 17.71m in the third round. In his kitbag was a tin of sardines, representing Christ's feeding of the 5000 and his own religious faith.

Joy on the face of Edwards as he wraps himself in the Union Jack after winning Olympic gold at Sydney 2000.

A year later, the pressure off him, he was to win the World Championship for a second time and in his final competitive season in 2002, he won gold at the Commonwealth Games and a bronze medal at the European Championships. He became a BBC presenter for Athletics and, until 2007 when he announced he had lost his Christian faith, its religious programmes. He is now an ambassador for the London 2012 Olympic Games and a member of the council of the European Athletics Association.

'I never ran to be famous. I only ever ran to see how fast I could run.'

# SALLY **GUNNELL**

**Sally Gunnell was the first British woman to win gold medals at all four major international Championships – the Olympic Games, World and European Championships and Commonwealth Games. She did it in the same event, the 400m Hurdles, but she was also a remarkably gifted all-round athlete.**

**Born:** 29 July 1966, Chigwell, England
**Height:** 1.67m (5ft 5in)
**Weight:** 58kg (127lb)
**Olympic highlights:**
1988: 400m Hurdles 5th
1992: 400m Hurdles gold; 4 x 400m Relay bronze

Gunnell grew up on her father's 300-acre farm in Essex, but instead of falling into the common sports of the farming family she was an athlete from the age of 11. At only 14 she was national junior Long Jump champion and at 16 she set a British record for her age for the seven-event Heptathlon.

Her course in athletics was finally set at the age of 18. She finished second that year in the national Heptathlon championships and third in the 100m Hurdles. In each she had the Olympic qualifying standard, but she was not selected for the 1984 Olympic team going to Los Angeles. That decided her to concentrate on a single discipline, the Hurdles. Her decision was proved correct within two years – by the age of 20 she had won the gold medal in the 100m Hurdles at the 1986 Commonwealth Games in Edinburgh.

Gunnell had good fortune as a teenager when Bruce Longden, coach to the 1980 Olympic Decathlon champion Daley Thompson, spotted her. His wife competed for the same Essex Ladies club as Gunnell, and he invited her to join his elite squad at Crystal Palace. The two were to stay together throughout her career.

Gunnell set a British record for the 100m Hurdles of 12.82 seconds early in the Olympic year of 1988, as well as a wind-assisted time of 12.8 seconds. It ranked her fifth in the world and would have been good enough to finish fourth in the Olympic Games, but she and Longden had decided instead that summer to bid for selection at the 400m Hurdles. 'There are ladies from Eastern Europe you are going to chase forever,' he said of the sprint event.

She achieved selection with a progress that was remarkable, beginning the Olympic year by winning the European Indoor Championships at 400m in a British record of 51.77sec. That set her up to break the British record for her new event four times during her first summer, culminating in a time of 54.03sec, which earned her fifth in the Seoul 1988 Games.

At the beginning of 1990 she beat Australia's Olympic champion Debbie Flintoff-King to win the Commonwealth 400m gold, and took the silver in the sprint Hurdles and a gold in the 4 x 400m Relay. But a midwinter event in the southern hemisphere played havoc with her winter training programme, and she performed poorly that summer in Europe.

That changed in 1991 after she was appointed British team captain. She broke her own British record for the 400m Hurdles twice, and again at the World Championships in Tokyo, but was rewarded only with silver behind Belarus's European champion, Tatyana Ledovskaya. The next year did not start auspiciously. She was beaten twice by Sandra Farmer-Patrick, an American many saw as favourite for gold at the Barcelona 1992 Games, but opinions changed after Gunnell's opening rounds at the Games. She won both, her semi-final result faster than the other race won by Farmer-Patrick. That meant her lane was inside her rivals', an ideal position to monitor their progress.

Farmer-Patrick had the lead until the seventh flight of hurdles but faltered, and Gunnell was well ahead by the ninth. Her time of 53.23 seconds was not even a British record but it was enough on that day to win by three and a half metres. 'I had visualized crossing the line so often, and tried to imagine what it would feel like, but it hadn't felt like this! I had got it all wrong. It was totally different,' she said of that triumphant moment in her autobiography.

For many, an Olympic gold is followed by anticlimax, a competitive year that shows the effects of celebrating its predecessor too much. Gunnell instead only became better and faster, winning every Hurdles race in preparation for the 1993 World Championships in Stuttgart. In the final there, she was not in the lead coming into the finishing straight and did not pass Farmer-Patrick until they were going over the final flight of hurdles. Both women broke the former world record but it was Gunnell who was given the verdict in a time of 52.74. It was the eighth time in her career that she had improved the British record.

Before her retirement after the 1994 season she won the Commonwealth Games gold, as well as gold in the 4 x 400m Relay, and became European champion, completing the perfect set of four titles – the first British woman to do so.

She was chosen as Britain's sportswoman of the year in 1992, 1993 and 1994 and the world athlete of the year in 1993. After her retirement, she worked for many years for BBC Television on its Athletics productions, while bringing up a family with her former athlete husband, Jon Bigg, in Sussex.

Opposite: Arms raised in triumph, Gunnell celebrates winning gold in the 400m Hurdles at Barcelona 1992.

# DAVID **HEMERY**

**Born:** 18 July 1944, Cirencester, England
**Height:** 1.87m (6ft 1in)
**Weight:** 72kg (159lb)
**Olympic highlights:**
1968: 400m Hurdles gold, 48.12sec WR
1972: 4 x 400m Relay silver; 400m Hurdles bronze

**David Hemery was a perfectionist, and in the rarefied atmosphere of the Mexico City 1968 Games, on 15 October he ran a race so perfectly that he won it in a time that broke the world record by a full seven-tenths of a second. 'I'd have been very disappointed if I hadn't won,' he said.**

If that suggests an immodest man, it cannot be further from the truth. Hemery was, as Sir Arthur Gold, president of the European Athletic Association, put it, quoting a line from Chaucer's *Canterbury Tales*: 'a verray parfit gentil knight'. Or as an American journalist of his time put it: 'The kind of British guy you only see in the movies'.

Tall, fair-haired and elegant, Hemery was almost Edwardian in appearance, a Corinthian figure and charming, polite and diffident of manner. Yet behind the appearance and personality were an iron determination and discipline. If he wanted something he worked at it until it was achieved. As he once said himself: 'Competition always fascinated me, even if it was just knowing that I could improve on the number of times I could jump on a pogo stick.'

He was competing in athletics by the age of nine. He was timed at school at the age of 11 running 440 yards in 1:08.70. But it was as a hurdler that he was to excel. Under the guidance of a 70-year-old Harrow School maths master named Fred Housden, he won the AAA junior title at 110m Hurdles at the age of 18, and at 21 the AAA and Commonwealth gold medals. Afterwards he judged that he would never be a fast enough sprinter to win global titles and focused instead on 400m Hurdles.

Hemery lived from 12 until 18 in Boston, Massachusetts, where his father worked, and he returned there to study at Boston University. He teamed up with coach Billy Smith, a hard taskmaster. 'Fred Housden taught me how to hurdle, Billy Smith to work and I added the third component, which is what's going on in the mind,' said Hemery. On that he became an expert, writing a PhD thesis that became a book, *The Pursuit of Sports Excellence*, and on which he based seminars that became his livelihood after Athletics.

Smith worked him hard in the hills around Boston and on sand dunes on its coast. He would ask Hemery to run up 30-metre sand dunes 35 times. No account was given to weather. Once when it was snowing heavily, Smith cleared a single lane of the track for Hemery's session to continue. 'Out there lies the road to Mexico,' he told him.

Hemery reckoned he enjoyed 60 weeks of non-stop hard work before the Mexico City 1968 Games, interrupted by a single week when he had flu. But he was able to race only once in 1967 – a 110m Hurdles race – and although he won the US National Collegiate title in a British record of 49.1 seconds in the Olympic year, he arrived in Mexico largely disregarded as competition. The three Americans in the event had all run faster, Geoff

Below: Gold-medal winner Hemery tops the podium at the medal ceremony after his amazing 400m Hurdles win at the Mexico City 1968 Games.

Opposite: Out front alone in lane six, Hemery closes in on Britain's first gold medal at 400m Hurdles for 40 years.

**'I was delighted that it was completed, that there weren't any pieces missing, that I hadn't let anybody down.'**

**Hemery,** on his gold at the Mexico City 1968 Games.

02

Hemery was part of Great Britain's silver-medal winning 4 x 400m Relay team at Munich 1972. From left to right, David Jenkins, Hemery, Alan Pascoe and Martin Reynolds.

Vanderstock setting a world record of 48.8 seconds in the US Olympic Trials.

Hemery and his British teammate John Sherwood each set British records in their semi-finals, identical times of 49.3, but again the Americans were faster, and the Germans Rainer Schubert and Gerhard Hennige had run European record times of 49.1. Because of this, Hemery was relegated to lane six, not a favourable starting position. He had run through every possibility in his mind so often that nothing like a lane draw concerned him. 'When I visualised the race in my head, it was in the greatest sensory detail. Even my heart rate and breathing rate would rise,' he said. 'I thought that if I ran my perfect race I could finish ahead of everyone.'

Hemery, as planned, was ahead early in the final. He broke the field by halfway – which he reached in an incredible 23.3 seconds – and increased his lead with every flight of hurdles. He won by eight metres, the widest margin of victory since the Paris 1924 Games, in a time of 48.12, an improvement on Vanderstock's record of 48.2 seconds. It was a time that no other Briton was to better for 22 years.

Hemery: first; the rest: nowhere, as it was reported at the time. 'It was like putting the last piece into a giant jigsaw; I was delighted that it was completed successfully, that there weren't any pieces missing, that I hadn't let anybody down,' said Hemery later. 'I had two emotions – the first was that I hadn't blown it!'

He received his gold medal, fittingly, from the last Briton to win the event 40 years earlier – Lord Burghley, the 5th Marquis of Exeter, an IOC member and president of the International Amateur Athletics Federation. Further honours were heaped on him. He was chosen as BBC TV's Sports Personality of the Year for 1968, and awarded the OBE in the New Year's Honours.

Incredibly, he took the immediate decision to abandon the event after just one full season at it. 'After winning the Olympic gold medal and breaking the world record it seems to me that you might only go back if you continued to specialise,' he explained. He decided that he had two other options: retire to coach or seek a fresh challenge in another event. 'I was only 25. I was too young to stop enjoying myself as an athlete,' he decided, and chose the mountain of a challenge in the 10-event Decathlon.

He succeeded in competing for Britain at the event but he was never going to be a threat to men with far greater physiques. His best score, in his second competition, was 6,893, which was not close to being competitive at international level. Injuries eventually persuaded him to abandon the challenge. Even then, rather than return to his best event, he went one step further back to the sprint Hurdles, an event in which he ultimately set six British records.

At the end of 1969 he won the silver medal at the European Championships and in 1970 retained his Commonwealth title, and won at the World Student Games. He did not compete during 1971, spending his time teaching at Millfield School in Somerset, and acting as director of an end-of-season Athletics meeting at Crystal Palace.

Not having run a single 400m Hurdles since his triumph in Mexico, it was on that event that he set his sights for the 1972 season, returning to Boston to train again under Smith. 'Everything is worth it for the Olympics. There's nothing else like it. I want the opportunity once again to struggle against myself,' he said. The motivation, though, was no longer to seek his limits. 'I just thought I ought to go on,' he said, and that was not enough to persuade him to train as he had in 1968.

He admits to having nursed negative images, like being beaten, and saying to himself 'just do your best'. 'I was fighting this concept that perhaps I was too old,' said Hemery. It was a self-doubt that was to destroy his chances at the Munich 1972 Games. He set a faster early pace than at the Mexico City Games, covering the first 200m in 22.8, but he lacked the endurance he had once had. To his surprise an unknown Ugandan, Jon Akii-Bua, was right beside him with 100m to go and surged ahead after the eighth hurdle. He was to break Hemery's world record in 47.82 with the Briton third in 48.52. Akii-Bua, ironically, was coached by a Briton.

Hemery blamed negative thinking. 'If you rehearse self-doubt, it will kill you,' he said, and he used it as an example in his subsequent teaching at Millfield School and in his seminars and motivational speaking.

He was to end his Olympic career by running a leg for Britain's team in the 4 x 400m Relay, in which they won the silver medal behind Kenya in a time that broke the British record and equalled the European record. He had completed a full set of Olympic medals. Amazingly, he had only contested the individual event that brought him his greatest triumphs in four seasons.

Hemery retired from Athletics immediately, recognising that the motivation had gone, but when the BBC invited him to take part in its series *Superstars* – a test across a spectrum of sports – he could not resist. He set about training himself again, and he was to win the series in 1973 and 1976. 'I love challenges,' he explained at the time.

He was elected the first president of UK Athletics in 1998 and chairman of the Confederation of British Sports. He became deputy chairman of Performance Consultants International and deputy-chairman of the British Olympic Association.

Hemery in action in the 400m Hurdles at the Munich 1972 Games. The Ugandan athlete John Akii-Bua (right) eventually took gold in the event.

# ALBERT **HILL**

**Born:** 24 March 1889, London, England
**Height:** 1.78m (5ft 10in)
**Weight**: 72kg (159lb)
**Olympic highlights:**
1920: 800m gold;
1500m gold;
3,000m team race silver

**Albert Hill has been largely forgotten nearly a century later, but his feat of winning the 800m and 1500m at the same Olympic Games in 1920 has never been equalled by another British man, and only by Dame Kelly Holmes among British women.**

Hill was a railway worker, operating out of Brighton and London Bridge stations before the First World War. He took up sport at the age of 15 when he left school, trying swimming and cycling before chancing upon athletics when he was invited to run in a local 880 yards race. He finished second and was smitten with running.

His first successes came in cross-country running. He won the North London junior cross-country title over five miles in three consecutive years. When he turned 20 in 1909, he finished fourth in the AAA four-mile championships on the track, and a year later he won the title.

He chose not to compete in 1912, apparently because of his marriage that year – he was to be married for 56 years – and so sacrificed any chance of competing in the Stockholm 1912 Games. War, during which Hill served as a wireless operator for the Royal Flying Corps in France, caused the cancellation of the 1916 Games and his only chance was to be the Antwerp 1920 Games.

Demobbed early in 1919, he returned immediately to training under the direction of Sam Mussabini, coach to a 1908 Olympic champion and later, more famously, to Harold Abrahams, who won the 100m in 1924. In his first competitive post-war season, Hill won a heat and final of the 880 yards, the one mile and an 880-yard leg of the medley Relay for his club, Polytechnic Harriers at the AAA Championships, all within the space of three hours.

That should have guaranteed him Olympic selection, and he chose not to run the one mile at the 1920 AAA Championships, assuming that confirming his form in the mile would be enough to convince selectors to name him in both events. Unfortunately, he was beaten into second place in the 880 yards by Bevil Rudd, a British-born South African.

Officials, assuming Hill was past his best at 31, named him only for the 1500m, but he complained to the AAA, saying a leg injury had hampered him. 'I well remember the strong argument I had with Sir Harry Barclay, the AAA secretary, because the committee was opposed to my attempting the 800m and 1500m. I was adamant and in the end he bowed to my argument,' said Hill later. He repaid them handsomely with his running in Antwerp.

That Olympic Games, held in spartan conditions in a war-devastated country, was difficult for the competitors. The British had to sleep on camp beds, and there were many complaints about accommodation and transport. Hill found himself delivered by lorry with wooden seats to his preliminary heats of the 800m! The timetable meant that he had to run five races in four days, some in wet weather conditions on a sodden cinder track.

So it was a Herculean effort, made more demanding for him when officials decided to put all the best runners in one heat to give the less

Hill, winner of the 800m and 1500m in 1920 and the only British man ever do that double at an Olympic Games.

able competitors a better chance of reaching the final. He survived that test and won a close 800m final with perfect tactical sense, passing the South African Rudd, who had won the 400m title, in the last 20 metres to win in 1:53.4, ahead of American Earl Eby. 'The most satisfying victory of my career,' he described it later.

The 1500m was harder for him, but his team captain Philip Baker said afterwards: 'While others were counting aches and pains and biting nails, Hill would have an early lunch and then sleep soundly for three hours.' There was driving rain on a track heavily marked by days of competition. But once he took the lead at the bell, accompanied by fellow Briton Philip Baker, Hill was never challenged. 'My races went as I expected,' he said with simple candour.

Hill won in 4:01.8, a half-second ahead of Baker and more than a second in front of the American Larry Shields, who won bronze. He remains to this day the oldest man ever to win the 1500m at the age of 31 years, 4 months and 26 days. Three days later Hill helped Britain to win a silver medal in the since-discontinued 3000m Team Race, finishing seventh himself.

The following year, his last, Hill won the AAA mile title again in 4:13.8, which broke the 32-year-old British record by three seconds and was less than a second off the then world record. He retired, taking up coaching.

He guided Jack London to a silver medal in the 100m at the Amsterdam 1928 Olympic Games and then, more significantly, the renowned runner Sydney Wooderson to world records in the 880yd and one mile distances during the 1930s. Hill and his wife emigrated to Canada in 1947 when their daughter married a Canadian, and he died there in 1969.

## 'My races went as I expected.'

Hill wins the 800m two metres clear of Earl Eby (third from left) and bronze medallist Bevil Rudd (right).

# KELLY **HOLMES**

**Born:** 19 April 1970, Pembury, England
**Height:** 1.64m (5ft 4in)
**Weight**: 55kg (121lb)
**Olympic highlights:**
1996: 800m 4th; 1500m 11th
2000: 800m bronze; 1500m 7th
2004: 800m gold; 1500m gold

**At the Athens 2004 Games Kelly Holmes became the first British female athlete to win two Olympic gold medals, and the first Briton since 1920 to achieve the golden double at 800m and 1500m.**

For Holmes, the best in life came late because of a succession of injuries that hindered her in the middle of her career, and robbed her of the successes that were expected of one so obviously talented. Not only did she win her Olympic gold medals at 34, but a Commonwealth Games gold medal, a World Indoor Championship silver and a World Championship silver all in her thirties.

Small and slight but immensely powerful, Holmes was a child prodigy born of a Jamaican father and English mother. Within a year of taking up the sport as a 12-year-old, she won the 1500m for her age group at the English Schools Championships. She was later to compete for Britain as a junior international athlete.

Holmes led for much of the 1500m final in Atlanta 1996 but it was Russian Svetlana Masterkova who took gold. It was a valuable learning experience for Holmes.

But turned her back on the sport to follow another of her dreams – a career in the British Army. At the age of 17 she signed up for the Women's Royal Army Corps and in the process gave up serious athletics. However, she did stay in good shape and played volleyball, won army judo titles and occasionally competed for her regiment at athletics – once running in the men's race because she was adjudged too good for the women's event – but only after she achieved the rank of sergeant as a physical training instructor did she resume athletic training with any serious intent.

It was watching the Barcelona 1992 Games on television at her army barracks in York that captured her imagination and prompted a return to competitive athletics. She saw a former rival, Lisa York, running for Britain in the 3000m in Barcelona. 'I thought, "Wow, I could be doing that. If she can do it ... surely I can." It gave me back a dream I had as a kid of running in the Olympics,' said Holmes years later.

Such was her natural talent and the high degree of fitness she had from training army recruits to the required levels that she was able to return to international competition within a year. She was coached again by the local coach in Tonbridge, Kent, Dave Arnold, who had advised her as a teenager when she first joined the local club. In only her second season of senior competition she won a silver medal in the 1500m at the European Championships in Helsinki, and gold in the Commonwealth Games in Victoria, Canada. A year later, in 1995, she won a bronze medal in the 800m and silver in the 1500m at the World Championships in Gothenburg.

The injuries that were to cause her so much distress during her career first affected her in the Olympic year of 1996. She was expected to be among the contenders in Atlanta in 800m and 1500m but it was discovered that she was running with a hairline fracture in her lower left leg. In spite of immense pain she managed to finish fourth in the 800m and reach the final of the 1500m, where she limped home in 11th place.

In 1997 she arrived as a favourite for the 1500m at the World Championships in the Olympic Stadium in Athens, the scene seven years later of her greatest triumph. She led the world rankings at the time by five seconds but on the first morning of the

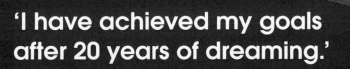

## 'I have achieved my goals after 20 years of dreaming.'

**Holmes,** after announcing her retirement.

Holmes's delight is apparent as she finishes the 1500m at Athens 2004 to complete the 800m and 1500m double – a feat never before achieved by a British female athlete.

Holmes won a bronze medal in the 800m at Sydney 2000 but coming after an injury-stricken run up to the Games, her joy is unrestrained.

Championships, in the first heat of the 1500m, her calf muscle in the same left leg that had fractured the previous year went into spasm and caused her Achilles tendon to rupture on the final lap. She managed to limp slowly to the finish but was registered in the results as 'Did Not Finish' because of how long it took her. By the time the final was run, Holmes was in hospital in Switzerland undergoing surgery.

'I was in the shape of my life. Not to be able to carry it through was heartbreaking,' she said at the end of her career in 2005, another occasion attended by serious injury. Indeed, she admitted in her autobiography that by 2003 she was so depressed by the injuries that she began to self-harm, and even went so far as to contemplate taking her own life.

Holmes was nothing if not tough mentally and each time she fought back. She took the 1998 season off to recuperate and by 2000 was fit enough again to win the bronze medal in the 800m at the Olympic Games in Sydney, and finish seventh in the 1500m. In 2001 she won another bronze at 800m in the World Championships, and in 2002 regained the Commonwealth title at 1500m and won a bronze medal at 800m in the European Championships.

At this point she became friendly with the outstanding middle-distance runner of her generation, Maria Mutola of Mozambique, three times world champion and the 2000 Olympic champion. Mutola invited Holmes to train with her and live at her house in South Africa, and Mutola's American coach, Margot Jennings, took over the planning of her training schedules.

That winter Holmes won a silver medal in the 1500m at the World Indoor Championships, and that summer, at the World Championships in Paris, seriously challenged her friend, overtaking her before the final bend of the 800m final. Mutola beat her in the end but Holmes's reward was another silver medal.

The two continued to train together for the Olympics, but after Mutola tripped into Holmes and fell in an indoor race in February 2004, they parted company. For the Athens 2004 Games, Holmes decided late in the day, while at Britain's pre-Games camp in Cyprus, to challenge for both middle-distance events, even though the finals were only five days apart. Ironically, there was an injury scare even then when she woke one morning with a pain in her left leg, only to discover she had been bitten by a 10cm-long centipede.

Holmes was a master tactician by this late stage of her career, but she took everybody by surprise in the qualifying heat for the 800m and in the final by running much of each first lap at the back of the field. Never did she set the pace or dictate to her rivals but allowed them to fight among themselves. Another veteran, American Jearl Miles-Clark, took command, with Holmes last of all for the first 300m. Eventually Mutola took the lead with 100m remaining to run, but as she did, Holmes followed her and passed her. It was the first time she had ever beaten Mutola and her winning time of 1:56.38 was the fastest she had run for nine years. At 34, she was the oldest ever competitor to win the gold medal in the women's two-lap race.

In the 1500m final, Holmes again remained at the back of the field. This time it was a Russian, Natalya Yevdokimova, who set the pace. Holmes was still in fifth place with half the final lap gone and only around the final curve did she sweep into the lead, pursued by the world champion, Tatyana Tomashova. She crossed the line, arms spread with a wide grin on her face, again the oldest winner of the event in its 32 years on the Olympic programme. Her time of 3:57.9 beat the British and Commonwealth record that had stood in her name for seven years.

The British team immediately honoured her achievement by inviting her to carry the Union flag at the Closing Ceremony, and when she returned to her home town, an open-top bus parade through her village of Hildenborough and the neighbouring small town of Tonbridge was watched by an estimated 40,000 crowd, the equivalent of the entire population.

Holmes was chosen as the BBC Sports Personality of the Year and the Laureus World Sportswoman of the year in 2004, but rather than retire from the track she decided to have one more season. Again, her plans were wrecked by injuries, and in her final race in Sheffield she trailed home last in the 800m. She announced her retirement with the words 'I have achieved my goals after 20 years of dreaming.'

Holmes, who had been made an MBE for her services to army sport in 1997, was awarded a DBE in the New Year's Honours list, entitling her to be known as Dame Kelly Holmes. She was by now putting her name and efforts behind a scheme to help other young British women to achieve the heights she had, a campaign she called 'On Camp with Kelly'.

Dame Kelly was elected president of Commonwealth Games England when Sir Christopher Chataway retired after 12 years in the role, and it was a reflection on her work with others that at the first Commonwealth Games afterward, four of the girls in her group were selected to run. She also took on a more political role, speaking on the value of sport at the Conservative Party Conference and becoming adviser to Boris Johnson, the Mayor of London, on how to make use of the 2012 Games as a sporting legacy for Londoners.

Holmes take the Union Jack on a lap of honour after winning the second of her gold medals – for the1500m – in Athens in 2004.

# DENISE **LEWIS**

**Born:** 27 August 1972, West Bromwich, England
**Height:** 1.73m (5ft 8in)
**Weight:** 74kg (163lb)
**Olympic highlights:**
1996: Heptathlon bronze
2000: Heptathlon gold
2004: Heptathlon DNF

**Denise Lewis was expected to have serious competition for the gold medal in the Heptathlon at the Sydney 2000 Olympic Games from the French athlete Eunice Barber, the world champion. In reality the most serious challenge she faced was the risk of physical injury. Her triumph was one of mind over body.**

Lewis, tall and physically striking, was a naturally gifted athlete, hugely promising from her early teens as a long jumper and hurdler, and well supported by her mother, Joan, a single parent and nurse. She won the English National Schools Championship in Long Jump twice, and her first international appearance for Britain in its junior team was as a jumper.

She began at her local club in Wolverhampton but her all-round ability was spotted by a Midlands schoolteacher, Darrell Bunn, who was one of Britain's best coaches of multi-events. She switched to Bunn's Birmingham club, Birchfield Harriers, where he schooled her from her mid-teens in a variety of events with the intention of her becoming a heptathlete, the seven-discipline event for the multi-talented. Her first competition saw her win the Midlands senior championship at 16.

A serious knee injury while competing for Britain's junior team as a long jumper and which required surgery took almost two years out of Lewis's competitive progress in her late teens. She then missed the Heptathlon qualifying score for the Barcelona 1992 Olympic Games even though she finished second in the National Championships, and she again missed the following year's World Championships.

Nobody was expecting too much at the 1994 Commonwealth Games. She was not Britain's number one and had not been selected for that year's European Championships. Most felt she would do well to finish in the top six. So there was genuine surprise when a javelin throw, which surpassed her previous best by six metres, led to a gold medal at the Games in Victoria, British Columbia.

She set her first British Heptathlon record to start the 1996 Olympic year and came away from the Olympic Games in Atlanta with a bronze medal, the one medal won by a British woman at those Games. It was more remarkable because she was in only sixth place after the first day's four events. A long jump of 6.32m, a massive javelin throw of 54.82m and a solid 800m in 2:17.41 on the second day elevated her to the podium and a score of 6,489 points.

The following year she won the silver at the World Championships, in 1998 she retained her Commonwealth title and won the gold medal at the European Championships and in 1999 she again won silver at the World Championships behind the Sierra Leone-born, naturalised Frenchwoman Eunice Barber.

Lewis went to Sydney for the 2000 Olympic Games with public expectations high. Just two months earlier, in Talence in France, she had set a new British and Commonwealth record score of 6,831. Unknown to the public, though, she had injured herself in the intervening weeks.

While training in Holland with her new Dutch coach Charles van Commenee, Lewis had experienced pains in her foot. A scan revealed damage to her Achilles tendon. Instead of training hard for the Games she spent the last few weeks enduring three sessions of physiotherapy every day,

Lewis in full flight in the Long Jump competition during the Heptathlon at Atlanta 1996 on her way to a bronze medal.

## 'Then the moment that will stay with me for the rest of my life – my name in lights. That's when it hit me.'

**Lewis,** after winning gold at Sydney 2000.

and arrived at the Olympic Stadium with her lower leg heavily bandaged.

Her medal chances suddenly seemed less than rosy, but Barber had problems of her own, only thinly disguised by a fine start which had her in first place after two events. Lewis, in contrast, had a poor High Jump, which dropped her to eighth place.

The turning point came in the Shot Put. Lewis had a fine throw of 15.55m which raised her to third place, while Barber could do no better than 11.27m and dropped back to eighth. After day one and four events, Lewis was third.

The second day began with Barber withdrawing from the competition after one Long Jump, but Lewis's own problems multiplied. Shooting pains in her foot hurt so much that they brought tears to her eyes. Before the next event, the Javelin, she needed the maximum dose of painkilling ibuprofen and her foot was heavily strapped. Her physiotherapist, believing she may have had a stress fracture in a bone, also put a felt pad in her shoe to ease the pain. Amazingly she was able to throw the javelin 50.19m to take the lead by 62 points and then run the 800m, strapped on both calves and one ankle. Russian Yelena Prokhorova ran more than six seconds faster but Lewis was sufficiently fast to hold on to first place by 53 points.

Lewis withdrew from the World Championships in 2001 because of illness and gave birth in 2002, but returned for one last Olympic Games in 2004. Not fully fit, she withdrew after the fifth event, while in seventh place, before announcing her retirement.

Twice runner-up in the BBC Sports Personality of the Year awards, her sporting achievements were recognised by her elevation to the Order of the British Empire in the New Year's Honours in 2000.

Above: Lewis begins her triumphant march to Heptathlon gold at Sydney 2000 with a time of 13.23 seconds in the first event, the 100m Hurdles.

# The Coe vs Ovett Era

**Rarely in the history of Olympic competition has a Games been so focused on two men in a single event as at Moscow in 1980. That Games, marred by boycott and politics, will be remembered forever for the exploits of Coe and Ovett.**

Seb Coe (no. 254) leads teammates Steve Ovett (no. 279) and Steve Cram (no. 257) in the final of the 1500m at the Moscow 1980 Games. Coe won, beating his arch-rival Ovett.

## 'It was the Moscow Olympics. It was the Coe-Ovett Olympics.'

*Steve Scott, American 1500m runner.*

The surnames are enough, like Torvill and Dean and Laurel and Hardy. Sebastian, known as Seb, was the smaller of the two, the university-educated son of an engineer who became his self-taught trainer; Steve, tall and powerful, was the enigmatic son of a Brighton market trader.

That they were both Englishmen in a golden decade for British Athletics made their rivalry more intense, yet they hardly knew each other and never met over the distance around which much of their fame existed – the mile. Indeed, in international careers lasting more than a decade, they only raced against each other a handful of times.

It was their two races in Moscow that defined a rivalry built up by the British media, as though Coe was the good cowboy in the white hat riding to showdown with the 'baddie' in the black hat, a parody of the truth about two men who were to become good friends in later life.

The rivalry began at 800m in 1978 at the European Championships. Coe was European indoor 800m champion and UK record holder. Ovett was UK-record holder over the mile and 1500m. So wary of each other's potential were they that tactically they handed the race to East German Olaf Beyer. Ovett finished second, Coe third.

In 1979, Coe set three new world records in 41 days, an amazing run of results. On 5 July, he beat the 800m record by a full second. On 17 July, he became the first man since Peter Snell to hold the 800m and one-mile records when he ran a mile in 3:48.95. On 15 August he improved the 1500m record to 3:32.03.

The following year, just minutes after Coe had set a fourth world record at 1000m in Oslo's Bislett Stadium, Ovett responded by bettering Coe's mile record in a time of 3:48.8 on the same track. Then 14 days later, with the Opening Ceremony of the Olympic Games in Moscow only four days away, he as good as equalled Coe's 1500m record with a time of 3:32.09.

Both men were entered by Britain for the 800m and 1500m. The furore surrounding the first meeting of their lives on the track on 26 July was such that Coe was met on arrival in Moscow by 400 journalists. Ovett, in contrast, refused to talk to the press. The popular consensus was that Coe would win the shorter race, Ovett the 1500m.

The 800m final was a slow, rough race which suited the more powerful of the two. Ovett was happy employing his elbows when he became boxed. Coe fought shy, running at the back of the field. Other runners complained later at Ovett's aggression but while Ovett pushed to second on the back straight and into the lead 70 metres out, Coe waited. But he waited too long. When he came finally at a sprint, it was to take only second place. Ovett won in a slow 1:45.40, more than three seconds slower than Coe's world record. Coe admitted he ran like a 'chump and a novice'.

Ovett now seemed the overwhelming favourite for the 1500m. He had the psychological edge and the knowledge that he was unbeaten in his last 42 races at the distance. In his semi-final his confidence was very evident as he found the time to wave to the crowd before crossing the line, while Coe, by contrast, actually struggled through his preliminary round.

What the media critics of Coe's earlier performance underestimated was his disappointment and the hunger it generated within him to put the record straight. Ovett followed Coe closely in the final but could not match his finishing kick, fading to third behind East German Jurgen Straub as Coe crossed the line with a ecstatic look of relief on his face. 'For the first time at 1500m I collapsed under pressure. I think Seb did the same in the 800m,' said Ovett.

Far from ending media interest in their rivalry, the one win apiece fuelled it. They raced each other constantly but on different tracks, each attacking the other's records. Ovett was first the next month, lowering Coe's 1500m record to 3:31.6 in Koblenz in Germany, while Coe came back in 1981 with another hat-trick of records, the 800m, 1000m and Ovett's mile record.

Seven days later, again in Koblenz, Ovett regained the record, but 48 hours later Coe had it back, breaking the mile record for a third time, a feat previously achieved only by the Swedes Gundar Haegg and Arne Andersson.

They were to meet again at the Olympic Games in Los Angeles in 1984 – when Coe won silver at 800m and gold at 1500m and Ovett ended in hospital – but never at their peaks. Injuries and illnesses in the meantime had taken their toll, and the greatest rivalry in British Athletics history expired without them ever racing outside of championships.

The podium places after the 1500m at Moscow 1980. Sebastian Coe won gold, Jurgen Straub of East Germany (left) silver and Steve Ovett bronze.

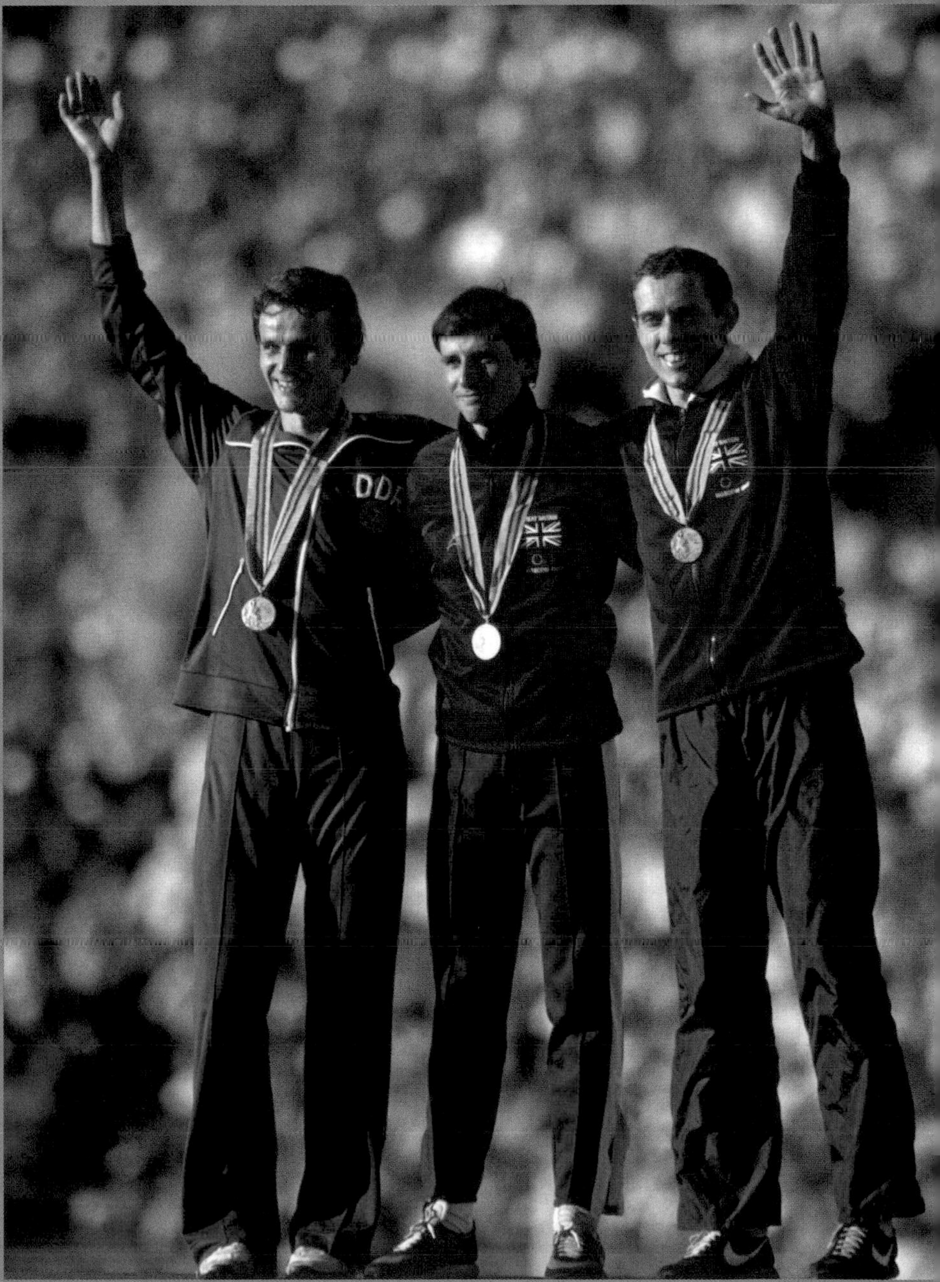

# ERIC **LIDDELL**

**Born:** 16 January 1902, Tientsin, China
**Height:** 1.73m (5ft 8in)
**Weight:** 68kg (150lb)
**Olympic highlights:**
1924: 400m gold; 200m bronze

**Eric Liddell's sporting life was immortalised in the fictionalised Oscar-winning movie *Chariots of Fire*, but in truth the reality of Scottish rugby's flying winger who won Olympic gold is even more fantastic.**

For dramatic purposes, movie scripwriter Colin Welland had Eric Liddell deciding on the Dover–Calais ferry, on his journey to the Paris 1924 Olympic Games, that he could not compete in the 100m because the heats were on a Sunday. Welland has another runner giving up his place in the 400m to accommodate Liddell.

Not true, but not entirely untrue. Liddell had given up any thought of running the 100m because of the importance of the Sabbath to him, but had done so six months earlier, when the timetable was announced. He had elected then to run only the 200m and 400m, and far from needing anybody's place, he was one of the favourites in the event.

Liddell was a sporting giant of his time. He won seven rugby caps as a winger for Scotland, while winning the first of five successive Scottish championships at 100 and 220 yards at the age of 19. He also won the two events at the AAA Championships in 1923, his time of 9.7 seconds for the 100m standing as a British record for 35 years.

Such was his brilliance as a runner that when he fell in a 440yd race in an international match against England and Ireland, losing 20 yards to rivals, he was still able to win. 'I don't like being beaten,' he said.

He retired from rugby union that winter to concentrate on training for his twin aim of competing in the 200m and 400m at the Olympic Games, and he earned selection when he won the 440yd at the 1924 AAA Championships.

At the Olympic Games he spent the morning of the 100m heats he might have run giving a sermon at a Scottish church in Paris. He won bronze in the 200m, and then improved his 400m best by more than a second in the semi-finals. Drawn in the outside lane for the final, where he was unable to see the opposition, he set off at a pace to exhaust a lesser man.

He reached halfway in 22.2 seconds, but rivals expecting him to tire were disappointed. His lead grew until he won by five metres in an Olympic, European and British record of 47.6 seconds.

A year later, after winning three more Scottish titles, he joined his father in China as a missionary, and he was to die there in a Japanese internment camp in 1945, aged 43.

## 'I don't like being beaten.'

Liddell crosses the line to win one of his gold medals at Paris 1924. He would have competed in the 100m as well but refused to do so on religious grounds as the race was held on a Sunday.

# DOUGLAS **LOWE**

**Douglas Lowe was the first man to successfully defend the 800m Olympic title four years after winning it. Yet when he won it for the first time in 1924, he had never won his own national title.**

**Born:** 7 August 1902, Manchester, England
**Height:** 1.83m (6ft)
**Weight:** 70kg (154lb)
**Olympic highlights:**
1924: 800m gold
1928: 800m gold

Lowe (left) shakes hands with the man he has just beaten in the 800m, Switzerland's Paul Martin. Lowe's victory came on his 22nd birthday.

In 1924, before that year's Olympic Games in Paris, Lowe finished second in the AAA 880yd to Hyla 'Henry' Stallard, and it was Stallard who went to the Games as favourite. His South African team-manager thought that Lowe could be beaten if a fast pace was set. In the 800m final, Stallard led for 700m but it was his undoing, because Lowe and two others passed him. Lowe won in 1:52.4 to break the British record set when another Briton, Albert Hill, won the Olympic gold four years earlier. It was Lowe's 22nd birthday. The next day, in a 1500m heat, Stallard suffered a stress fracture in a foot bone but, insisting on competing in the final, he beat Lowe into fourth place to win bronze.

Lowe finally won his first AAA Championship in 1926 in a race that became famous as one of the great classics of British middle-distance running. Stamford Bridge was packed with 27,000 spectators to see the return to the championships of the Germans, banned since 1918, including Dr Otto Peltzer, the German champion at three distances.

Lowe chose to make the pace himself, covering the first lap in 54.6 seconds and staying ahead as Peltzer challenged on the back straight. Finally, Peltzer overtook to win in a world-record time of 1:51.6. Lowe reckoned that Peltzer's greater speed had been created by running one-lap races, so adopted the strategy himself for 1927. He even won his first AAA title at 440 yards.

Peltzer was favourite at the Amsterdam 1928 Games but was eliminated in the semi-finals after suffering an injury. Instead it was Lowe, with a devastating burst of acceleration, who won by eight metres over Swede Erik Bylehn, in an Olympic record time of 1:51.8. Typical of his era, Lowe wrote a letter to Peltzer that said: 'The British half-milers who have competed with you in the past feel duty bound to send you their deepest sympathy for the injury that prevented you from showing your best form in the Olympic Games.'

He was determined to ensure that Peltzer had another chance against him, and it came 19 days later in a meeting in Berlin. Lowe ran the fastest time of his life in a British record time of 1:51.2 to beat Peltzer by exactly one second. Honour satisfied, he retired from competition immediately.

# STEVE **OVETT**

**Born:** 9 October 1955, Brighton, England
**Height:** 1.83m (6ft)
**Weight:** 70kg (154lb)
**Olympic highlights:**
**1976:** 800m 5th; 1500m semi-final
**1980:** 800m gold; 1500m bronze
**1984:** 800m final; 1500m DNF

**Steve Ovett was the first of three British runners who were to rewrite the record books in the period when Europeans dominated middle-distance running. He set five world records at the 1500m and one mile and won the Olympic 800m gold medal in 1980.**

Ovett, tall and rangy, was a naturally gifted runner who had successes at every event from one lap to 5000m. His first, in winning the English Schools Championships when he was 14, was at the 400m and displayed the turn of speed that was to be his trademark in devastating finishes at longer distances later in life.

He was willing to try any events in those days, even Long Jump – his best was 6.28m aged 15 – and High Jump as a teenager. He won a silver medal in the English Schools Senior Cross-country Championships and yet sprinted to the AAA Youth Championship for 400m, and set a record for the distance for a British 16-year-old of 48.4 seconds.

His international breakthrough came in 1973 when he won the 800m at the European Junior (under-20) Championships, and at senior level a year later when he won the AAA championships and finished second in Europe's senior championships. In 1976, still only 20, he won both 800m and 1500m at Britain's Olympic selection trials. At the Montreal 1976 Games he finished fifth in the 800m final, but failed to qualify for the final of the 1500m, which was won by New Zealander John Walker.

The following summer he beat Walker over one mile in London, and then at the World Cup in Düsseldorf beat him over 1500m with a blistering final 200 metres. It made him the world number one at 1500m for the first time. He confirmed that status in 1978 when he won the European title at 1500m after taking a silver medal at 800m in a British record time, one place ahead of Sebastian Coe, now looming at home as his most serious rival. He also set his first world record at two miles, completing a collection of performances that had him voted the BBC Sports Personality of the Year.

By the time he and Coe met again, at the Moscow 1980 Games, Coe had set the first of his succession of world records and Ovett had set two of his own, beating Coe's record for one mile and equalling his record for 1500m. He had won 42 straight races at 1500m or one mile since 1977, and was favourite to win over the longer distance.

The reverse of everybody's expectations – and his own – was to happen. Ovett won the 800m with Coe second, while Coe responded by winning the 1500m with Ovett third. A month later Ovett broke the world record for 1500m.

In 1981 Ovett suffered a bizarre defeat in Oslo, where the American Tom Byers, who had been asked to pace a 1500m race, got so far ahead of those he was meant to pace that he won, with Ovett second. But in August that year Ovett broke the mile record in a time of 3:48.4. His start to the 1982 season was delayed by a strange training accident, in which he ran into church railings near his home while out running. It prevented three races in Britain that had been scheduled between Coe and Ovett, and he did not compete that year in the European Championships or Commonwealth Games.

It was not the end of his record breaking, but many believe he was never the same force again. He was fourth in the 1500m at the 1983 World Championships, a race won by the third of the outstanding Britons, Steve Cram. Three weeks later came the final world record of his career, a 1500m in 3:30.77 in Rieti, near Rome.

His final Olympic Games, in Los Angeles in 1984, were a huge disappointment for him. He suffered bronchial problems because of the smog associated with the LA air quality, and collapsed on the track at the end of the 800m semi-final after qualifying as the last man for the final.

In the final, he struggled to complete the race, finally finishing last, and ended up being taken to hospital in an ambulance. He spent two days there but returned to the stadium to qualify for the final of the 1500m. His condition worsened and he stepped off the track on the final lap, unable to get his breath. Again he was taken to hospital, the last act in an Olympic Games that would not go his way.

The final flourish of his career came in Edinburgh in 1986, when he won the gold medal in the 5000m at the Commonwealth Games. He qualified for that event at the 1987 World Championships, but only finished 10th and retired. He became a television commentator for ITV before emigrating to Australia, where he works for global television companies.

Years later, Ovett characteristically played down the importance of what he had achieved. 'If people want to look back in 100 years at someone who could run around a track in three and a half minutes, and if they think that's wonderful, then that's fine. I've enjoyed it, it was great fun.'

**'I thought, "You're Olympic champion – what was all the fuss about?" It was, in the moment after winning, a bit of a disappointment.'**

**Ovett,** after winning gold at Moscow 1980.

The strain shows on Ovett's face as he nears the finish of the hotly contested 800m final he won at Moscow 1980.

# ANN **PACKER**

**Born:** 8 March 1942, Moulsford, England
**Height:** 1.69m (5ft 6in)
**Weight:** 58kg (127lb)
**Olympic highlights:**
1964: 400m silver; 800m gold WR

**Ann Packer ran only the seventh 800m race of her life at the Tokyo 1964 Games, and broke the world record to win gold. It was also her last race. She retired immediately at the age of 22 to marry Robbie Brightwell, the captain of Great Britain's men's Athletics team at the 1964 Games.**

Packer (no. 55) wins gold at Tokyo 1964. A natural champion, she won easily.

Packer had always been a good athlete but was not serious about it until it was almost too late. She won the England Schools 100-yards Championships when 17. She tried Long Jump and won the women's National Championships, but was still then running sprints and sprint Hurdles, and it was not until 1962 that she took the sport seriously.

The turning point came when she was selected to compete for Britain in that year's European Championships, a complete surprise to her. 'I never dreamt for one moment that I would get in the team. I even wrote to the British selectors pointing out I hadn't done the qualifying time,' she said. But determined to justify their faith in her, she ran a personal best time of 24.2 in Belgrade to qualify for the final and helped Britain's 4 x 100m Relay team to win a silver medal.

That year she also ran in the Hurdles for England at the Empire Games but, now working hard at her training, she made the greatest breakthrough in 1963 when she attempted the 400m. She only did so because there were no sprints on the programme at a meeting in Reading, but having run 55.9 seconds, she tried again and progressed to 53.3 seconds by the season's end.

She was to go to Tokyo in 1964 as a favourite for a medal at 400m, like her fiancé Robbie Brightwell in the men's event. Indeed, both thought they could win gold, although neither thought anything of Packer's chances in the two-lap event. She had run it for the first time only in May that year.

In the 400m, Brightwell was disappointed to finish only fourth and Packer just as unhappy to finish second, even though she had run a European record time of 52.2 seconds. Her chances in her secondary event looked less favourable when she ran only 2:12.6 in her heat. 'I was clueless,' she admitted. But in the final she swept into the lead 70 metres from the line to win by five metres in a world-record time of 2:01.1. 'It was so easy, I couldn't believe I'd won,' she said.

She married Brightwell two months later and neither ever raced again. They went on to have three sons, two of whom played professional football for Manchester City.

**'It was so easy, I couldn't believe I'd won.'**

# MARY **PETERS**

**Mary Peters, affectionally known throughout Athletics and her adopted province of Northern Ireland as Mary P, began competing as a child, but her success did not come until her thirties. After a decade of international disappointments, she won the hearts of the German crowd at the Munich 1972 Games.**

**Born:** 6 July 1939, Halewood, England
**Height:** 1.73m (5ft 8in)
**Weight:** 68kg (149lb)
**Olympic highlights:**
**1964:** Pentathlon 4th
**1968:** Pentatlon 9th
**1972:** Pentathlon gold

Her father built her a long jump pit in their back garden for her 16th birthday after she had completed her first Pentathlon, the five discipline event for versatile women athletes. A year later he laid concrete for a shot put circle. At 18 she was one of only four women athletes in Northern Ireland chosen for the 1958 Commonwealth Games in Cardiff.

There was no Pentathlon on the programme, so she competed in the Shot Put and High Jump without success. When she returned to Belfast, there was a letter waiting that changed her fortunes. A local man, Buster McShane, was starting a weightlifting class and invited athletes to join.

Peters did so, and within three years McShane took the coaching of her Athletics events. In 1964 she won selection for the Olympic Games in Tokyo, where the event was included for the first time. She finished fourth. She was unsuccessful in the Shot Put and High Jump at the 1966 Commonwealth Games and again in the European Championships. Worse followed for her at the Mexico City 1968 Games, when she finished only ninth in the Pentathlon after hurting an ankle before the competition.

Her first gold medal was won in Edinburgh when the Pentathlon was included in the programme of the Commonwealth Games. Peters was 31 years old and she knew that the Munich 1972 Olympic Games would be her last chance. She gave it everything from the start, opening with a personal-best performance in the Hurdles of 13.3 seconds, and achieving another personal best in the Shot Put to take a slim lead.

It was the High Jump that won the crowd over to her side, even though her main rival was the West German Heide Rosendahl. Peters sailed over the bar until 1.71m, when she failed twice. After succeeding at the final attempt, she blew kisses to the crowd. Eventually she took a huge lead with another personal best of 1.82m, and had a lead of 97 after the first of the two-day competition.

Rosendahl, fifth overnight, soared to second when she jumped a massive 6.83m in the Long Jump. It meant that Peters had to run her best 200m to have any chance, and hope the German was not too far ahead of her. She did, and Rosendahl finished just 10 points behind her, the equivalent of a 10th of a second. Peters's score of 4,801 was a world record.

A fund to celebrate her win was raised by a local paper in Belfast, and she asked that it should be spent on a new track for the city, which was named after her. She continued competing for two more years, winning a Commonwealth Games gold for a second time, and later became manager of the British team for five years.

Peters sprints away from the blocks in the 200m in the Pentathlon event at Munich 1972. She won gold in her third appearance at the Games.

## 'What would I like people to say of me? That she did more than win an Olympic gold. She put something back.'

# MARY **RAND**

**Born:** 10 February 1940, Wells, England
**Height:** 1.73m (5ft 8in)
**Weight:** 61kg (134lb)
**Olympic highlights:**
1960: Long Jump 9th; 800m Hurdles 4th
1964: Long Jump gold WR; Pentathlon silver; 4 x 100m Relay bronze

**Mary Rand, the most complete all-around athlete in the history of British Athletics, was the first British woman to win an Olympic title in a Track and Field event when she took gold in the Long Jump at the Tokyo 1964 Games. She was also the first saddled with the sobriquet Golden Girl.**

There was almost nothing Rand (née Bignal) could not do at some level. She represented her country in 10 different events and set 19 individual national records in four different events. She began as a schoolgirl high jumper and ultimately set a world record while winning the Long Jump at the Olympic Games.

The daughter of a Somerset bakery worker, Rand failed her 11-plus but was given a scholarship to a high-fees independent school because of her sporting prowess, and blossomed there. By the age of 17 she was representing Britain as a high jumper and a year later set her first British record in the five-discipline Pentathlon.

Rand in action in the Long Jump competition that she went on to win at Tokyo 1964, with a world-record leap of 6.76m.

That same year, 1958, she won a silver medal in the Long Jump at the Commonwealth Games and was fifth in the High Jump, and later came seventh in Pentathlon at the European Championships. She became the first British woman to reach 20 feet in the Long Jump and in 1959, still in her teens, was chosen as Britain's sportswoman of the year after beating the all-powerful Russian women in the Long Jump and the Hurdles in Moscow.

She went to the Rome 1960 Games as favourite for the Long Jump, and justified it when she led the qualifying competition with a British record of 6.33m, the third longest ever. But in the final, nerves got to her. She could not get her run-up right, twice running through the pit, and failed to finish among the six competitors allowed three more jumps. She eventually finished ninth.

She was a creditable fourth in the Hurdles but returned to Britain labelled a flop. 'If I felt that winning the Hurdles semi-final and getting fourth in the final was some sort of compensation, I was fooling myself. I'd come for the Long Jump and I'd failed,' said Rand in her autobiography. 'Nothing could completely take away the sick feeling.'

She married an Olympic sculler, Sydney Rand, and had a daughter, Alison, but returned only four months after the birth to win bronze medals in Long Jump and sprint Relay at the 1962 European Championships. She enjoyed a glorious 1963, with a share in a world Relay record, but her career reached its zenith in the Olympic year of 1964 in Tokyo.

She was so versatile that she achieved the qualifying standard in six events. In one of her best, the Hurdles, she had to drop out because of a clash in the timetable but, perhaps significantly, she was not to go to this Olympics as favourite in any event. Russians were ahead of her in both Pentathlon and Long Jump.

She led the Long Jump qualifiers again, but this time put it together in the final with the greatest series of jumps ever accomplished in a Games. Four surpassed her personal best, and the worst of them would have won the silver medal. The best, her fifth, was a world record of 6.76m, the first time the imperial distance of 22 feet had been exceeded. Incredibly, she had done it jumping into a 1.69 metres per second headwind. Rand was not familiar with the metric system, so had to run back to her kit bag to get a copy of the day's programme to look up the world-record distance before she knew the magnitude of her achievement. 'I'm just relieved, so grateful, that I'm not coming home a flop, no one has to say, "Hard luck, Mary" this time,' she said.

Three days later she won a silver medal in the Pentathlon with a British record of 5,035 points, becoming only the second woman to exceed 5,000. The first, Russian Irina Press, beat her by 211 points, but Rand had beaten her in three of the five disciplines. It was Press's shot put, which scored 384 points more, that made all the difference. Rand then helped Britain's women to win a bronze medal in the 4 x 100m Relay, completing the perfect set of Olympic medals from the Games and earning herself that year's BBC Sports Personality of the Year, and an MBE in the New Year's Honours list.

She won the Long Jump again at the 1966 Commonwealth Games but retired when an injury prevented her winning selection for the Mexico City 1968 Games. She had by then won 10 national titles in four different events, and raised the British Long Jump record on 11 occasions – from her first record of 6.19m in 1959 to 6.76m – and the Pentathlon on six occasions. She had also set British records at 80m Hurdles and at 100 yards.

Her marriage to Rand ended in divorce and she married an American, Olympic Decathlon champion Bill Toomey, in 1969 and moved to California. They also divorced but she continues to live there, now as Mrs Reece.

'It wasn't a painful decision, retiring,' wrote Rand in her autobiography *Mary, Mary*. 'It was hardly a decision at all. It was as if I'd been in about three different whirlpools at once, spinning me different ways, and one of them had stopped.'

**'I'm just relieved, so grateful, that I'm not coming home a flop, no one has to say, "Hard luck, Mary" this time.'**

**Rand,** after winning gold at Tokyo 1964.

Right: Rand also competed in the Pentathlon at Tokyo 1964. She won silver, to add to her gold in the Long Jump.

# TESSA **SANDERSON**

**Born:** 14 March 1956, St Elizabeth, Jamaica
**Height:** 1.68m (5ft 6in)
**Weight:** 72kg (158lb)
**Olympic highlights:**
1976: Javelin 10th
1980: Javelin 19th
1984: Javelin gold, OR
1988: Javelin 21st
1992: Javelin 4th
1996 Javelin 14th

**Tessa Sanderson, who became the first Briton to win a throwing event at the Olympic Games in 1984, tied the world record for Athletics when she competed at a sixth Games in 1996, at the age of 40.**

Sanderson, born of Ghanaian ancestry in Jamaica, grew up in the English Midlands. She enjoyed athletics as a hobby but was only inspired to take it seriously after watching Mary Peters on television winning Olympic gold at the Munich 1972 Games. After competing in junior Pentathlon, she finally began her international career as a Javelin thrower when she finished fifth in the 1974 Commonwealth Games at the age of 17, the same year in which she was to finish 13th in the European Championships.

Her first Olympic Games was in Montreal in 1976 and her first international medal was a silver at the 1978 European Championships, the same month she won the first of three Commonwealth Games gold medals, achieved over a 12-year period.

She went to the Moscow 1980 Games as one of the contenders for gold, but had a horrible day in the qualifying competition. Her first throw was short of 50m, a distance she would normally have reached without a run-up and almost 20m below her best. Her two other throws failed to register a legal distance, and the competition ended with her in tears in the stadium tunnel.

Another Briton who did not qualify for the final was the younger Fatima Whitbread. Out of that day grew a great rivalry that became the women's version of Coe and Ovett, but with a spear – sometimes bitter, always intense and exciting for British crowds. They were to have 45 meetings, with Sanderson winning 27, but while she won Olympic

**'I won it for myself and my coach, but I can hold my head up and say, "Hey, Britain, this is for you, too."'**

**Sanderson,** after winning gold at Los Angeles 1984.

Below: Tessa Sanderson competing in the Javelin Throw at Los Angeles 1984, just one of six Olympic Games she appeared in.

Sanderson is all smiles after winning gold with a throw of 69.56m at Los Angeles 1984.

and Commonwealth gold, only Whitbread won World and European titles and set a world record.

Sanderson's greatest moment came at the Los Angeles 1984 Games. Coincidentally, Mary Peters, her original inspiration, was her team manager and among the first to congratulate her when she emulated her winning performance. Sanderson had missed out on a medal in fourth place at the 1983 World Championships when the Finn Tina Lillak won in her nation's capital, Helsinki, with her final throw, a world record. In the Olympic competition, Sanderson took the lead with a first throw of 69.56m, an Olympic record. Lillak's second effort fell only 56cm short, but the attempt also caused a stress fracture in her right foot and she was unable to continue.

Sanderson's throw was good enough to win but Whitbread's fifth throw moved her into the bronze-medal position, putting two Britons on the podium. She won at the European Cup in 1991 at her sixth attempt but never again won an Olympic medal, coming closest in 1992, when she finished fourth in her fifth Games. This was a then record for a British woman athlete.

A month later she won at the World Cup, 15 years after her debut in that event, and announced her retirement, aged 36. She had won nine National Championships, set 10 British records and increased the national record from 56.14m to 73.58m. Five of these records had also been Commonwealth bests, and she had competed 57 times for her country. She also set two Commonwealth records at Heptathlon in 1981 and ran the 400m Hurdles in a respectable 60.46 seconds.

Sanderson went on to make a living in television, working on Sky News and later on ITV and the BBC, but her career as an athlete was not over. In 1996 she was persuaded to return to the Javelin in an effort to raise money for a hospital charity, with a goal of making her sixth Olympic Games.

She set world over-40 records at 58.18m and 60.64m with the first two throws of her comeback meeting at Bedford, and later improved the record three times, eventually reaching a distance of 64.06m. She also competed at a seventh European Cup. Ranked 20th in the world that year, and as number one in Britain, she was chosen for the Atlanta 1996 Games.

She did not reach the final – her best of 58.86m in qualifying was only enough to place her 14th – but her appearance equalled the record sixth Games of Romanian Discus thrower Lia Manoliu. Her 20-year span at the Olympic Games also equalled the record of Manoliu and British high jumper Dorothy Tyler.

She retired again after those Games, but continued her association with sport when she was appointed vice-chair of Sport England, a position she filled from 1999 until 2004. She was made a Commander of the British Empire for that work, and heads an academy in the London Borough of Newham that seeks to produce talented young sports people to compete at the London 2012 Olympic Games. She also serves on the board of the Olympic Park Legacy Company.

In 2010 she married another former Olympic competitor, Judo star Densign White, now sports director of the European Judo Union.

# DALEY **THOMPSON**

**Born:** 30 July 1958, London, England
**Height:** 1.84m (6ft)
**Weight:** 88kg (194lb)
**Olympic highlights:**
1976: Decathlon 18th
1980: Decathlon gold
1984: Decathlon gold
1988: Decathlon 4th

**Daley Thompson was arguably the greatest multi-event athlete of all time and without any doubt the greatest among Britons. Four world records, two Olympic gold medals, three Commonwealth gold medals and world and European titles are testimony to that.**

Daley Thompson, in a characteristic display of certainty in his own ability, sent a postcard to the Californian home of American double Olympic Decathlon champion Bob Mathias before the Olympic Games in Moscow in 1980. It read: 'I'm going for three!' He was never to achieve a hat-trick of Olympic golds because of injury but Thompson, even when he continued competing well into his thirties, never stopped believing that he could.

The son of a Nigerian father and Scottish mother, he was named Francis Morgan at birth but known to all as Daley, a contraction of the African word Ayedele, meaning 'joy come home'. Thompson took to athletics when he was sent by the London Education Authority at the age of eight to a boarding school in Sussex as a difficult child. He won most school events by great margins and was as talented among his contemporaries when the school sent him to a local club in Haywards Heath.

His future as a decathlete – a competition in which points for performances in 10 individual elements of sport are totalled to decide a winner – was settled with his first attempt in 1975, but the pivotal moment had come a year earlier, when he failed to do well in three individual events at the AAA Youth Championships. Down in the dumps and thinking of quitting for football, he met a London club coach, Bob Mortimore, who encouraged him to keep trying.

He joined Mortimore's club in east London, Essex Beagles, where he added some technique to his natural speed and trained harder than anybody. Mortimore sold him the idea of multi-events and his first was in Wales, less than four months after he began training for it. He was 16 – below the minimum age in a competition for those over 19 – but officials allowed him to compete and he won, setting a record score for a British 16-year-old. 'After the first day I thought, "I could be the best at this,"' said Thompson.

Everybody who witnessed the competition claimed later that they knew they were seeing a future Olympic champion. Not only did he have the fundamental speed and build necessary for multi-eventing, but he had the temperament of a champion, a winning mentality and a refusal to be beaten. And, he admitted later, the good fortune to have his two best elements – the 100m and Long Jump – starting every Decathlon.

Within a year he was selected by Britain for his first Olympic Games in Montreal after he had set the first of 10 British and Commonwealth records of his career. He was to be the youngest competitor in the event. He finished 18th with 7,330 points but Bruce Jenner, the American who won the gold medal with a world-record score, tipped Thompson to win next time.

Jenner's perspicacity was proven only a year later when Thompson set a world junior record and won gold at the European Junior Championships. He also finished fifth in the individual Long Jump at those championships, and in 1978 won the first of his Commonwealth Games gold medals, his first senior title. It elevated him to the status of favourite for the European Championships a few weeks later, but Thompson lost it on the Javelin and finished runner-up to the Russian Aleksandr Grebenyuk. It was to be his last defeat for nine years.

Thompson finally moved to the top of the world rankings in May 1980 at an international Decathlon

Thompson easily clears the bar in the High Jump event of the Decathlon at the Moscow 1980 Games. He went on to clear 2.08m.

**‘I thought I was the best decathlete in the world but you have got to prove it to them. The Olympics is the place to do that.’**

**Thompson**, after winning his first gold at Moscow 1980.

Thompson in action during the Long Jump element in the Decathlon at Los Angeles 1984. Thompson won gold with a world record score of 8,847 points.

competition in the Austrian town of Gotzis. He looked destined to break the world record Jenner had set at the Montreal 1976 Olympic Games by a comfortable margin after nine events, but dawdled through three laps of the 1500m before breaking into a final lap sprint. Ultimately he broke Jenner's record with a score of 8622 by only five points. A telegram from Jenner congratulated him.

He lost his record within weeks to Guido Kratschmer, whose German team boycotted the Moscow 1980 Games, as did the United States, the home nation of many of Thompson's serious rivals. So while Thompson's first Olympic gold medal was won against lesser opposition, he at least did it by a respectable margin of 164 points.

Thompson reclaimed the world record in Gotzis in 1982 when another German, Jurgen Hingsen, emerged as a serious rival. Thompson quickly put him in his place in Athens at that year's European Championships by again breaking the world record. He finished the year by winning his second Commonwealth Games gold in Brisbane – becoming the first man ever to hold Olympic, World, European and Commonwealth titles simultaneously – and it was no surprise that the British public voted him BBC Sports Personality of the Year.

Thompson remained something of an enigma, never one to respect the media or traditions. He turned up to receive his award at the live BBC event, where others were in evening dress or suits, wearing his tracksuit. He rarely talked with the press, declining one request from a journalist who was an Olympic champion himself when the man could not name the 10 events in the Decathlon in the right order. He turned down a chance to carry England's flag at the Opening Ceremony of the 1982 Commonwealth Games, saying, 'I am not a tourist.' As *The Times* wrote: 'This is not a man destined to become a sports diplomat.'

He was, though, a great athlete. 'All I ever wanted was to be the best. I didn't enjoy fame,' said Thompson, and he built on natural speed with great technique taught to him initially by national coach Bruce Longden, and later the chief national coach Frank Dick.

That was honed on the prodigious amounts of physical effort he put into his training. Often he would work for eight hours in a day. He always trained on Christmas Day, he said, because his rivals would not be. It was psychological as much as physiological with him, gaining an edge. 'The most competitive sporting animal I have ever come across,' said Frank Dick.

In 1983 Thompson lost his world record to Jurgen Hingsen, and within weeks, at the first World Championships, his friends feared he might lose to

**Thompson in the Pole Vault in the Decathlon at Los Angeles 1984. He vaulted 0.5m higher than his rival Jurgen Hingsen, which gave Thompson the points advantage he needed to take gold.**

him again in Helsinki because he had injured himself three weeks earlier when he slipped on a wet floor in a supermarket. Typically, Thompson made no mention of it outside his tight circle of training partners, and he rose to the challenge by beating Hingsen to the title.

'Daley is extreme at everything, but you have to be extreme to get that power when you need it,' Hingsen said of him years later. 'He always had an enormous will to win. He was an absolute winner. Even if the situation was very difficult he could always find a way out. He always had the potential to combine his motivation with his dynamics.'

Again in 1984, Hingsen – nicknamed Hollywood by Thompson because he had a girlfriend from the American movie capital – came to the year's main event, the Olympic Games in Los Angeles, as the reigning world-record holder, only to be overwhelmed. 'Daley is a Stalinist. It's not enough for him to win; he has to mentally destroy his opponent,' said Sebastian Coe, Olympic champion and Thompson's close friend.

Thompson's performance surpassed the German's in the 100m and Long Jump, the first two events. Hingsen pulled back in Shot Put and High Jump and the critical moment for Thompson came on the second day in the seventh event, the Discus. Thompson fluffed his first two attempts, while Hingsen threw an impressive 50.82m. Unless Thompson improved on his final throw, Hingsen would take the lead for the first time in the competition. Thompson, as mentally strong as he was physically impressive, threw his third attempt 46.56m to keep the lead.

Hingsen became ill during the next event, the Pole Vault, performing poorly and the rest was a formality for Thompson. He had only to run the final event, the 1500m, in a slow 4:34.98 to break Hingsen's world record, but eased off and missed surpassing it by two points. Only one other man – the American Robert Mathias – had ever before won a second Olympic Decathlon gold.

Two years later, the IAAF, the world governing body, re-examined the finish photo of the 110m Hurdles, and discovered that Thompson had been quicker in the 110m Hurdles. As a result, they awarded him a share in Hingsen's record, his fourth world record. The score of 8,846 points was to remain the greatest of his career.

Thompson, unbeaten in 12 Decathlons over seven years, lost his unbroken sequence at the 1987 World Championships in Rome when he was suffering a groin strain. He could finish only ninth. Again not fully fit, a year later he was fourth in his fourth Olympics, missing a bronze medal by 22 points, and in 1989 he needed a bone growth removed from his knee.

He tried, aged 33, to qualify for his fifth Games in 1992, but it ended in embarrassment for him. Before a handful of people watching an event at Crystal Palace especially arranged for him to attempt to score the qualifying standard, he failed even to finish the first event, the 100m. His career ended at that point, with him carried from the track injured.

Thompson continued his close involvement with the sport after his retirement from competition, working to inspire the young. He was to become a key figure in the creation of the Laureus Academy, a sponsored global organisation which works promoting sport in developing countries, and an ambassador for London 2012 after the British capital city won the right to host the Olympic Games.

Thompson always liked the 1500m the least of the ten Decathlon elements and the exertion shows in his expression as he nears victory at Moscow 1980.

# ALLAN **WELLS**

**Born:** 3 May 1952, Edinburgh, Scotland
**Height:** 1.83m (6ft)
**Weight:** 86kg (190lb)
**Olympic highlights:**
1980 100m gold; 200m silver; 4 x 100m Relay 4th
1984 4 x 100m Relay final; 100m semi-final

**Allan Wells is the only Scot to win the 100m at the Olympic Games, and was the first Briton to win the event for 56 years. Yet he began his athletic career as a long jumper, inspired by an Olympic champion.**

Allan Wells was a Scottish jumper who, in mid-career, changed to the sprints and became one of the most successful sprinters Britain ever produced, and its first Olympic 100m champion since Harold Abrahams.

Wells, the son of a blacksmith, won the Scottish junior Triple Jump title in 1970, and went on to clear a respectable Long Jump distance of 7.32m. He was inspired by 1964 Olympic Long Jump champion Lynn Davies, but seeing the Jamaican Don Quarrie win both sprints at the 1970 Commonwealth Games in Wells's native Edinburgh persuaded him to experiment with sprinting as a sideline.

Arms raised, Wells celebrates winning Britain's first gold medal in the 100m for 56 years at Moscow 1980.

It was not an immediate success. He was 24 before the coaching of Wilson Young, a former professional sprinter, produced in him his first sub-11-second time for 100m, and it was not until the early months of 1977 that he won his first national title, the 60m Indoor Championships.

It was a year later, in 1978, after his 26th birthday, that he broke into the world rankings, equalling Peter Radford's 20-year-old British record for 100m, then reducing it to 10.15 seconds. A month later he won the 200m gold at the Commonwealth Games after setting a new British record in the heats, as well as winning a second gold in the 4 x 100m Relay and a silver in the 100m. The next year he twice broke the British 200m record.

Wells was now coached by his wife, Margot, herself an international sprinter. He had never used starting blocks, preferring the old-fashioned crouch position, but a change in IAAF rules forced him to adapt to them for the Moscow 1980 Olympic Games. How well he adapted showed in his heats, when he set a British record of 10.11 seconds. It was to remain his career best.

In the final, he just edged out pre-Games favourite, Silvio Leonard of Cuba. 'I saw Leonard, he was right up there, and I thought to myself, 'Well, I'm going to get a medal anyway, I'll bloody well make a dive for the line and give it everything,"' said Wells. The two men shared the same time of 10.25 seconds, the slowest winning time for 24 years, but Wells was awarded the gold. At 28, he was the oldest winner in Olympic history.

Wells, the first sprinter to wear cyclists' thigh-length lycra shorts, was in lane seven for the 200m

**'Take every superlative there is, roll it into one and you have an idea of the elation I felt when I won in Moscow.'**

**Wells,** after winning gold at Moscow 1980.

final, one lane inside Italian Pietro Mennea, the world-record holder. Wells started furiously, closing the stagger to Mennea before the straight and leading out of it, two metres in front of Leonard, with Mennea third. Wells lost his lead only in the final 10 strides, losing by 0.02 seconds to the Italian in a time of 20.21 seconds, despite a desperate lunge for the line.

To complete his Games, Wells ran the anchor leg as the British quartet finished fourth in the 4 x 100m Relay, a remarkable collection of first, second and fourth places for a man not chosen for his country's national team four years earlier.

Many thought Wells fortunate. The American sprinters had been absent from Moscow because of the United States boycott of the Games. But just a few weeks later at a post-Olympic meeting in Cologne, Germany, he emphatically set the record straight when he beat the best of the US team – Stanley Floyd.

In 1981 he was again clearly the world's number-one sprinter. He won the European Cup and World Cup and finished first at 200m and second at 100m in the inaugural IAAF Golden Sprint, taking the overall title. A year later he was still at the peak of his powers. He won the gold medal in the 100m in the Commonwealth Games in Brisbane, then shared gold in the 200m when he dead-heated with England's Mike McFarlane.

In 1983 he was fourth in both 100m and 200m at the World Championships, and qualified for a second Olympic Games in 1984. Now 32 and eliminated from the 100m in the semi-finals, he helped the British quartet reach the final of the 4 x 100m Relay.



He wanted to bow out at the 1986 Commonwealth Games in his home city of Edinburgh – the event at which his thoughts had first turned to sprinting – but injury caused him to miss selection. He was fit in time to score one more notable victory, over the new Commonwealth champion, Canadian Ben Johnson, the same month.

Later that summer he finished fifth in the 100m and 200m at the European Championships in Stuttgart before announcing his retirement. Long since living in Guildford in Surrey, he was to devote himself to a career in the engineering department of the University of Surrey.

Wells dips desparately at the line at the end of the 100m at Moscow 1980. The race ended in a photo finish – Wells's dip was enough to clinch the gold medal.

# The Olympic Walkover

**The White City Stadium provided no shortage of entertainment at the London 1908 Olympic Games. On one day in July the winner of the Marathon, the Italian Dorando Pietri, was disqualified for receiving assistance. The next day saw the only gold medal won by walkover in the history of the modern Games.**

British and American athletes and officials gather on the track at the scene of the disputed Men's 400m final at the London 1908 Games.

Wyndham Halswelle, a London-born army officer of Scottish descent, would probably have won the gold medal in the 400m in Athletics anyway. He was the favourite going into the Games, a formidable runner who achieved a feat unique in the history of Scottish athletics when he won the 100yd, 220yd, 440yd and 880yd championships on the same day.

Two years before London 1908, at the Intermediary Games in Athens (now not recognised as an official version of the Games), Halswelle won silver in the 400m behind an American, Paul Pilgrim. In 1908, he set a world record for 300m and a British record for 440yd.

In the preliminary round in London, he strolled to victory in the fastest time in the 16 heats, and in the semi-finals he won – according to the official Games record – by 12yd, and set an Olympic record of 48.4, a full second faster than the next best in that round.

Halswelle qualified for the final against three Americans: Williams Robbins, John Taylor and John Carpenter. The race was to be run on a three-laps-to-the-mile cinder track in which the finishing straight was 165yd long but, significantly, there were no marked lanes.

The same had been true in Athens two years earlier, where Halswelle had been the victim there of interfering tactics by Pilgrim. These were allowed under the rules of the US governing body, the Amateur Athletic Union, but not by those of England's Amateur Athletic Association (AAA), and it was England's rules that the International Olympic Committee had decreed for all Athletics events in 1908. In the programme on the day of the 400m final, the rule was printed for all to read: 'Any competitor wilfully jostling or running across or obstructing another competitor so as to impede his progress shall forfeit his right to be in the competition...'

Alerted by events in Athens two years earlier, officials also placed judges at various points of the track to see that the rule was obeyed. It was not. Robbins cut across Halswelle 50 metres from the start. Halswelle dropped back and came around Robbins and Carpenter on the first bend, but immediately Carpenter moved to block him.

One judge reported later that Carpenter kept his right shoulder sufficiently in front of Halswelle to force him wider, to a point where he was eventually running only half a metre from the outside edge of the track. Roscoe Badger, a vice-president of the AAA and an umpire, cried 'foul', ran onto the track and called for the finish tape to be broken.

Four judges consulted, declared the race void and posted a chalked sign that read 'No Race'. They ordered the final to be rerun 'in strings' – lane ropes – two days later, on 25 July, the day after the Marathon, but with Carpenter disqualified from competing.

Robbins and Taylor refused to be part of the rerun out of sympathy for Carpenter. Halswelle was pressured into competing by AAA officials. So he ran alone at a controlled pace in a respectable time of 50 seconds.

Halswelle, a lieutenant in the Highland Light Infantry, graduate of the Royal Military Academy at Sandhurst and the grandson of a general, decided to retire from the sport, aged 26. He ran only once more to fulfil an obligation to the Glasgow Rangers Sports at the Ibrox Ground in Glasgow a few weeks later.

The 400m contributed to a diplomatic row between Britain and the United States that had been caused by disputes in many sports over interpretation of rules. The US Olympic Committee, alone among nations present at the Games, did not write to thank the British Olympic Association, and the contemporary criticism in US newspapers led to a book being published in response in Britain, giving its side of the story.

The ramifications for Halswelle's sport and for the Olympic Games were more lasting. The IOC decided that local rules should never again be used. By the next Games, an international athletics federation – to be known as the International Amateur Athletic Federation – was being formed, in order to create a uniform rule book.

One of those earliest rules was that the 400m should be run in lanes marked on the track. That 'No Race' in London was the last at an Olympic Games where there was any opportunity for interference from other competitors.

Halswelle lived long enough to see that change but not for many years more. Promoted to captain in 1911, he died in the First World War, killed by a sniper's bullet at Neuve Chapelle, France, in 1915, aged 32. He was elected posthumously to the Scottish Sports Hall of Fame, but he should be best remembered for his greater contribution to future harmony within the sport.

Wyndham Halswelle crosses the line to win gold in the 400m. Halswelle was the only competitor in the race after the American team boycotted a rerun.

# TIM **BRABANTS**

**Born:** 23 January 1977, Chertsey, England
**Height:** 1.89m (6ft 2in)
**Weight:** 88kg (194lb)
**Olympic highlights:**
2000: K1 1000m bronze
2004: K1 1000m 5th
2008: K1 1000m gold; K1 500m bronze

**Tim Brabants took up Canoeing because his mother tired of his relentless energy. He was to become unquestionably the greatest British canoeist in Olympic history, the first to win an Olympic medal and the only one to have won an Olympic gold.**

What makes Tim Brabants's achievements more remarkable is that he has done it while qualifying as a medical doctor and working in hospitals between Games. He admits he owes it to the support made possible by the British World Class Performance programme funded by the National Lottery. Before those days, the elite sports competitor would work or study by day, train in the evening and be permanently tired. It was not a good recipe for achieving success, either in the day job or the sport.

Since he qualified as a doctor in 2002, Brabants has instead taken 18 months to two years off after each Games to pursue medical ambitions. It means that he gets further and further behind his contemporaries in his profession, but just manages to make up time in his sport.

He took up Canoeing as a 10-year old when his mother, anxious to find something to burn the energy of a restless boy, signed him up for a Canoeing course during his summer holidays. He continued at university in Nottingham, where he earned selection for the British squad.

At the Sydney 2000 Olympic Games his bronze medal in the kayak 1000m came as something of a surprise. It was Britain's first medal of any colour in the sport and came only with a tremendous burst of acceleration over the final 250 metres.

It persuaded him that he could win gold four years later in Athens, and he was encouraged further when he became the first Briton to win the European championship in 2002. Indeed, after the qualifying round in Athens, in which he paddled to the fastest time ever recorded for 1000m, 3:24.412, he became the favourite to win gold. Unfortunately, Brabants had mistimed his effort. He could not sustain it in the final and finished fifth.

Below: Brabants was content with a bronze medal in his first Olympic Games at Sydney 2000.

Opposite: The joy is obvious after Brabants wins gold at his third attempt, at the Olympic Games in Beijing 2008.

Had he won, he might have retired to concentrate on medicine, but instead he took 18 months out to work in accident and emergency departments. He returned to the water to train on the Thames in early 2006, a double sacrifice because his wife's job in Nottingham meant that they were kept apart. That year he won a silver medal at the world championship, and in 2007 he became the first Briton to win the world championship in his speciality event.

That triumph was to mean he would go to Beijing as favourite for gold, a pressure he felt in Athens only in the 24 hours after his qualifying race. It was a real pressure – Britons had won 17 gold medals already at the Games, and the nation was expecting more – but this time he got his timing right. 'We'd been discussing all year how to race an Olympic final,' said Brabants.

His tactic was to put in a fast start. Flanking him were Adam van Koeverden, the Canadian who had been runner-up to him at the world championships the previous year, and another co-favourite, Erik Larsen of Norway, and he wanted to put the pressure on them. 'After two strokes I knew victory would be mine,' said Brabants.

Van Koeverden kept with him for 500 metres before Larsen tried to reel him in over the second half. Both men thought Brabants's rapid start would leave him fading at the finish, but Brabants never lost his lead. 'Easy to say now I've won that I always knew, but I really did know,' he said. 'Those first two strokes told me it was going to be my day.'

Those who finished behind him marvelled at the manner of his victory. 'I've watched the guy on video and YouTube, and I'm honoured to get a bronze medal behind him,' said Ken Wallace, the Australian who came in third.

Brabants's career was not finished at the Beijing Games. He had paddled to his fastest 500m time at a World Cup race earlier in the summer in Poznan – his 1:35.8 was the second-fastest ever – and fancied his chances at the shortest sprint for a gold. As it was, he had to settle for his second bronze medal.

At the age of 31, with a medical career already years behind those of his contemporaries, many men would have called it a day on the water. Brabants, inspired by three medals and the thought of a home Games in London, decided he wanted one more go at it. 'In a sense it's much more useful trying to save life than winning the 1000m at the Olympic Games. But the feeling I have got now is, you get greedy – medal fever,' he said.

So, he took time out to return to medical duties, working at the Queen's Medical Centre in Nottingham where he had trained. After 18 months he tossed away the white coat and was back paddling. In 2010, aged 33, he showed how little he had lost when, in his comeback season, he won a silver medal in the 1000m at the world championships.

**'After two strokes I knew victory would be mine. Easy to say now I've won that I always knew, but I really did know.'**

**Brabants,** after winning gold at Beijing 2008.

# NICOLE **COOKE**

**Born:** 13 April 1983, Swansea, Wales
**Height:** 1.67m (5ft 6in)
**Weight:** 58kg (128lb)
**Olympic highlights:**
2004: Road Race 5th; Time Trial 19th
2008: Road Race gold

**Nicole Cooke was the first Briton to win a gold medal at the Beijing 2008 Olympic Games – a triumph not just for the British team but also for Cooke, the first woman from Britain to win a gold medal in Road Cycling. It was a very different story from her first Olympic experience.**

For Nicole Cooke, winning an Olympic gold medal was the fulfilment of an ambition she had first mentioned publicly as a girl at just 11 years of age. 'What do you want to do next?' she was asked after winning a cycling race against boys. 'Win an Olympic gold medal,' Nicole's mother reported her daughter as saying.

She had been given her first bike as a Christmas present when she was six. Very soon she was riding tandem with one of her parents on their holidays – her brother rode tandem with the other parent – and her father, a former competitive cyclist, allowed her to accompany him on her bike on the hilly ride from her Welsh village to her school, where he taught physics.

Eventually, she became so good that she asked to be allowed to train alone. 'I get cold waiting for you at the top of hills,' she told him, and by now she was beating all the other local women in races. Her parents decided to take summer holidays in Holland, so she could race against better opposition there. Soon she was becoming the youngest ever to win major titles: among her laurels were the senior British Elite Road Race championships at only 16 and the British cyclo-cross championship when 18.

Cooke (left) crosses the line in the pouring rain to win the Women's Road Race, Britain's first gold medal at Beijing 2008.

# 'We did it, it was perfect. It's a dream come true.'

**Cooke,** after winning Olympic gold at Beijing 2008.

Her breakthrough year was 2001, when she won the world junior championships in Road Race, Time Trial and Mountain Bike, as well as the British senior road championship. A year later, still only 19, she won the gold medal in the Road Race at the Commonwealth Games in Manchester.

She became a professional for the 2002 season, winning several major continental races, and the following year won three races on the World Cup circuit and the overall title. The next year, Olympic year, began badly with rehabilitation from the effects of two crashes, one in collision with a police outrider, and keyhole surgery on her knee.

It meant that she did not race for eight months, but in her comeback competition she won the British Road Race title, and the next month the Giro d'Italia, the youngest ever to do so and the first British woman to win a Grand Tour event. She was seen as among the favourites to win the 126km Road Race at the Athens 2004 Games, but sadly she crashed and, despte remounting, finished fifth.

By 2005 she was regarded as one of the leading professionals on the continental scene, taking a silver medal in the Road Race at that year's world championships. In August of 2006 she made her status official when she became world number one on the UCI world rankings for the first time. That year she also won the *Grande Boucle* – the women's Tour de France – the overall World Cup series again, and retained her ranking until near the end of 2007.

2006 was to end badly for her. Another knee injury forced her to miss the final World Cup race, when she was leading in defence of her title. The title instead went to Holland's Marianne Vos, who also took Cooke's world Road Race title when the Welsh woman was unable to defend it. Cooke said later in an interview that she considered retiring at that point.

Instead, she was reinvigorated by a move to a new British team, using bikes designed by Chris Boardman. After winning the *Grande Boucle* again in 2007, 2008 was a vintage year. She became the first woman to win the Olympic gold and the world championships in road racing in the same year.

Cooke's triumph in Beijing was Britain's 200th gold medal at the Olympic Games. She won in torrential rain – 'a bit like home in Wales,' she said – despite losing contact with four riders in a breakaway bunch when she took the final turn cautiously because of the wet road. However, in the final sprint in the Juyongguan Pass by the Great Wall of China she made up the gap, letting out a shriek as she crossed the line in first place. 'There were so many emotions that just came out at once,' she said.

Her achievements were recognised with an MBE in the New Year's Honours list, and she became the Sunday Times Sportswoman of the Year, but 2009 was a quiet year for her, not helped when her professional teams lost their backers. She looked on target to regain her world title in 2010, but when poised before the final sprint to the line, she hesitated and three rivals swept past her.

There is no doubt, however, that there is not a British rider, male or female, who has ever matched the achievements of this cyclist, who has won titles in the Olympic Games and world championships, two Tours de France and the Giro d'Italia.

Cooke shows off the gold medal she won at Beijing 2008, to add to the astonishing list of professional *palmares*.

# CHRIS **HOY**

**Born:** 23 March 1976, Edinburgh, Scotland
**Height:** 1.86m (6ft 1in)
**Weight:** 92kg (203lb)
**Olympic highlights:**
2000: Team Sprint silver
2004: 1000m Time Trial gold
2008: Team Sprint gold; Sprint gold; Keirin gold

**Chris Hoy was a successful BMX rider and oarsman, but it was his career as a track cyclist that was to lead him to become the first Briton for 100 years to win three gold medals at a single Olympic Games, and the first racing cyclist ever to be knighted.**

No Briton had achieved the feat of three gold medals in a single Games since a swimmer, Henry Taylor, did so at the London 1908 Olympic Games. Not since those same home Games had Britain won more than the 19 gold medals won at Beijing 2008.

Unquestionably, Hoy is the greatest track cyclist Britain has ever produced and one of the greatest the world has seen, but what made Hoy's hat-trick more remarkable was that none of the three he won were in the event he won four years earlier in Athens. The UCI, the world governing body, had eliminated that event, the 1000m Time Trial (the Kilo), from the Olympic programme a year later to accommodate the Keirin, an oddity created for the betting market in Japan. So Hoy, who had never ridden it, retrained and re-educated himself and came to Beijing to win, as one of his three, the Keirin.

Hoy's physique was what people first noticed about this man hewn from the granite of his native Edinburgh. 'To say he is built like a brick outhouse does not do justice to an outhouse,' wrote one journalist. In massive thighs he had the power that gave him the astonishing speed that few could match on the wooden oval circuits of Track Cycling.

Olympic champions, though, are more than a perfect frame. Mind is as important as body. What came with the physique of Hoy was a competitive aggressiveness utterly suited to sprint events. He began cycling after being inspired by the BMX bikes ridden in the film *ET – The Extra-Terrestrial.* He raced a BMX bike until he was 14, eventually becoming

Right: Hoy in action in the Keirin, one of the three events at Beijing 2008 in which he won gold medals.

Opposite: Hoy is ecstatic after winning the Men's 1000m Time Trial at Athens 2004, his first Olympic gold.

**'Everyone asks me, "Who is my sporting hero?" thinking I'd choose someone from history. And I say, "Chris Hoy." He's an inspiration, a legend.'**

Victoria Pendleton,
Sprint gold
medallist, Beijing 2008.

# The London 1908 Games

**The modern Olympic Games began at Athens 1896 and were successful from the start. By the time the fourth version of the Games was due to be held, Paris and St Louis had both been hosts, before passing the baton to London in 1908.**

Rome had been chosen initially as the host city for the fourth modern Olympic Games, but it had pulled out due to financial constraints. London stepped in to fill the gap at short notice, despite being fourth choice.

But the London 1908 Games are seen today as a significant turning point in the Olympic Movement, a surprising success in spite of its organisers having had only 20 months in which to build a new 68,000-seat stadium and plan for 24 sports and 106 events.

Indeed, it was the partnership the newly created British Olympic Association formed with the Franco-British Exhibition that was fundamental to the Games' success. The exhibitors advanced a reported £60,000 to build what became the White City Stadium in west London and paid other costs.

Even so it needed a public subscription launched by newspaper proprietor Lord Northcliffe, which raised around £16,000 to fund the organisation of the Games.

The sports at those Games would have seemed odd to today's Olympic spectator. Motorboating took place on Southampton Water. Polo, Rackets, Real Tennis, Tug of War and, most oddly, Ice Skating were contested.

The timetable would also seem a far cry from the modern format. The first event took place in April, the last in October. One was postponed by six weeks to suit the convenience of the Duke of Westminster.

The London 1908 Games brought many innovations to the modern Olympic Games. For the first time gold medals – and replicas in silver and bronze – were presented. And they were solid gold, unlike today's gold medals, which are gold-plated.

For the first time there was a system of entry for competitors through national teams chosen by National Olympic Committees, although the restriction on the number of athletes each nation could enter in an event was generous. In some it was as many as 12.

With national teams, unfortunately, came nationalism. There were disputes even at the Opening Ceremony when the American flag bearer refused to dip the Stars and Stripes when

The men's 100m final gets underway at the London 1908 Games. South Africa's Reggie Walker (far right) won in a world record-equalling time of 10.8.

The Marathon at the London 1908 Games saw the streets of Eton lined with spectators and Union flags. The Italian Dorando Pietri crossed the line first but was controversially disqualified.

passing King Edward VII and the Swedes threatened a walkout because their flag was not flying at the stadium. Passions between the Athletics teams of Britain and the United States became so strained that relations between their National Federations were broken off after the Games.

The Games did not enjoy the best of fortunes in other respects. The weather for the main events in July was worse even than in the usual English summer. Rain fell heavily much of the time, forcing some of the Lawn Tennis at Wimbledon's All England Club to be played indoors. But a sudden heat wave drew a crowd of 90,000 for the final day.

The Games had its moments, though, and its genuine heroes. Most famous to this day remains the Marathon because of the disqualification of the Italian Dorando Pietri, who was first to reach the stadium.

Exhausted by the 26-mile, 385-yard course from Windsor Castle on a hot, humid day, he was soon at the point of collapse. Doctors revived him, only for him to fall again and again. By now American John Hayes had also entered the stadium but officials carried Dorando across the line ahead of him. The American complained and Dorando was disqualified, but such was the emotion generated by his efforts that he became a celebrity and was presented with a special gold cup by the Queen.

Britain, as host nation with the largest team, dominated proceedings. They won all four Rowing events at Henley and all weight divisions in Boxing. In the pool, which was simply a 100-yard-long tank erected within the stadium, Briton Henry Taylor won three gold medals, and only in Athletics did the British cede dominance, to the Americans. Indeed, several of Britain's seven gold medals were won in that sport by Irishmen, whose country was then still part of Great Britain.

The British also won the Tug of War, but only after the United States team withdrew in protest complaining that the studded heavy boots of the Liverpool Police team gave them an unfair advantage. Ultimately the City of London Police team won gold, although hardly within the amateur spirit of the times because they had been given leave to train together for five months before the Games.

The lessons learned in 1908, detailed in an honest report of its deficiencies by the British Olympic Association, led to changes that guided future Olympic Games. For London, the legacy was the White City Stadium, which was to remain the home of British Athletics until the end of the 1960s.

# BEN **AINSLIE**

**Born:** 5 February 1977, Macclesfield, England
**Height:** 1.83m (6ft)
**Weight:** 95kg (209lb)
**Olympic highlights:**
**1996:** Laser silver
**2000:** Laser gold
**2004:** Finn gold
**2008:** Finn gold

**Ben Ainslie is Britain's most successful Olympic sailor, second only to the Dane Paul Elvström as the most successful of any nationality and the only man ever to be chosen as the World Sailor of the Year three times.**

When Ben Ainslie moved to a new school in Cornwall, he was bullied. 'I discovered in sailing the one thing I am good at, a way out of it,' he said years later.

It is ironic, then, that Ainslie the sailor was to be described by *The Times* as a 'mobster in a dinghy'. Bullying rivals with intimidating sailing tactics became a strategy he employed to effect on many occasions. He recalls a rival who became so angry with him that he boarded Ainslie's boat to exchange words.

Ainslie, off the water in his home at Lymington in Hampshire, is often described as modest and self-effacing, and was even shy when he was younger. He rewrote the final chapter of his own autobiography because he thought his ghostwriter had made him sound arrogant by over-egging his achievements.

Below: Ainslie (left) leads Brazil's Robert Scheidt on his way to gold in the Men's Laser class at the Sydney 2000 Games.

Opposite: Ainslie at Sydney 2000. He moved up to the heavier Finn class for Athens 2004 and beyond.

On the water, in contrast, he is famous for sailing as close to the rules as he does the wind, employing every advantage at his disposal. 'My greatest strength is that I never give up,' he says of himself on his personal website. His second great strength is a competitiveness that has earned him the respect of his fellow sailors.

A classic example of his refusal to settle for second best came at the Sydney 2000 Olympic Games on the waters of the city's famous harbour. Ainslie was thirsting for revenge. He had been beaten into second place in the Laser class as a 19-year-old at his first Games at Atlanta 1996 after a titanic struggle with Brazilian Robert Scheidt, a sailor as dominant in his age as Ainslie was to become.

Scheidt, who led Ainslie by only two points going into the final race in 1996, had employed a cunning tactic against his youthful rival. After four false starts, officials raised the black flag, indicating that all boats jumping the gun at the next attempt would be disqualified. So quite deliberately Scheidt false-started, knowing it would entice most of the field to follow him rather than yield an advantage. Twenty boats did, including Ainslie's, and the double disqualification of the two leaders left Scheidt with the gold medal.

That began an intense rivalry between the two men. Scheidt won the 1997 and 2000 World Championships; Ainslie won in 1999. At Sydney 2000, the competition came down to the final race. This time Scheidt led Ainslie by nine points going into the race and, because of the discard system, and Scheidt's superior second-worst score, Ainslie could only win if the Brazilian finished outside the top 20.

So Ainslie set out to ensure that would happen, harassing Scheidt before the start and causing him to incur a penalty of a 720-degree turn for crossing the line early. From that point, Ainslie sailed to cause Scheidt maximum frustration, keeping ahead and taking his wind so completely that by the first mark the two were 90 seconds behind the rest of the fleet and three minutes behind the leaders.

At one point the two boats collided and at the finish line Scheidt was one place from his objective. He filed two protests, one about Ainslie's tactics at the start and another about the collision. The judges

‘I guess I am fortunate that I am still very passionate about winning.’

dismissed the first and adjudged Scheidt the guilty party in the second, disqualifying him. So Ainslie was the winner of the gold medal by a margin of 13 points. He had gained his revenge for his loss in 1996.

'It was an amazing feeling, and hard to describe in so many ways. I was very aggressive, with plenty being said between the boats. That was the most intense thing I have ever done,' admitted Ainslie.

The two men were to become friends. 'Robert Scheidt is the sailor I respect most in the world and I look back on those five or six years when we were pushing each other to such a high level as the making of my Olympic career. I modelled myself on him, looked at how he sailed, how he handled himself on and off the water. I set myself the task of learning his technique and getting to his level.'

Ainslie's background marked him for a life on the ocean waves. His father had skippered an entry in the Whitbread Round the World race in 1973, and he had his son in an old, heavy dinghy when he was eight after the family's move to Cornwall. He was competing in races aged 10 and at 12 took part in his first international race. He finished 37th but his progress was relentless.

By 1993 he was World and European Champion in the Laser Radial, a version of the Olympic-class Laser with a smaller mast and sail area suitable for lighter, usually younger, sailors. Two years later in the Olympic-class Laser he became World Youth Champion, his final step before his own Olympic debut a year later.

By 2000, Ainslie was bored with the Laser class. Having achieved his ambition of matching Scheidt in Olympic competition, he looked for a fresh challenge, leaving the Lasers for Scheidt to win the class again in Ainslie's absence in 2004. The Briton instead set about putting on 15 kilograms in weight to enable him to handle the far heavier Finn class boats, 4.5 metres in length and 126 kilograms in

Ainslie's move to the Finn class for Athens 2004 paid dividends as he celebrated his second gold medal at an Olympic Games.

weight. To do so he was consuming 5000 calories a day and maintaining a weight-training programme.

So rapid was his progress that he won the Finn Gold Cup – the de facto World Championship for the class – only two seasons after entering the class. He was to become the first to win the Cup for a fourth successive year in 2005 and won for an unprecedented fifth time in 2008.

His performance in the Olympic regatta in Athens was not dissimilar to that in Sydney. Again it ended with a highly tactical race in which Ainslie knew that his lead was such that he needed only to finish no more than 15 places behind a friend, Spaniard Rafael Trujillo, to be certain of gold. Typically, instead of trying to win, he simply followed Trujillo, ensuring that he finished just one place behind him.

He had begun the regatta disastrously and was in 19th place after the first day, having been disqualified from the second race following a protest by French sailor Guillaume Florent. Ainslie's response was characteristic of his competitiveness. He was to finish in the top four in the next eight races – four wins, two seconds, a third and a fourth. Success still left him frustrated that he had not enjoyed the satisfaction of winning gold by triumphing in the last Olympic race.

He was to put that right in 2008. So comprehensive were his preparations that he spent every moment he could in the Chinese port where the Olympic Sailing regatta would be held, getting to know its currents and its light winds. In one competition there in 2006, he won nine of the 11 races in the regatta.

When it came to the Olympic regatta, he was so far ahead of American Zach Railey before the final race that the gold would be his if he finished no more than six places behind him. The old Ainslie would have done only what was necessary. Instead he went for the victory, winning so comfortably that Railey said afterwards: 'Ben is the best dinghy sailor the world has ever seen.'

Ainslie himself described it as the most fulfilling of his three Olympic successes. 'In some ways this was the best of my gold medals because there was so much expectation coming into the event and conditions on the water were so difficult,' he said of Chinese waters, where winds were so light it was difficult to get any speed out of the heavy Finns.

Ainslie's third Olympic gold and fourth medal overall surpassed the achievement of Rodney Pattisson's two golds and three medals, making him Britain's most successful Olympic sailor at his fourth Olympic Games in total. 'When I was a kid, my generation all looked up to Pattisson and we were in awe of what he achieved. It seems a little surreal to be in the position I now am,' said Ainslie, by then a veteran of 31.

Ainslie was not only a fine dinghy sailor. Between Athens and Beijing he was second helmsman for New Zealand's America's Cup entry, and in 2009 he was contracted to skipper Britain's potential America's Cup challenger Team Origin as helm. He translated his skills to the larger boats, winning the World Match Racing Championship in 2010 and becoming ranked world number one in the big boat class.

The gold medals keep coming for Ainslie as he wins again, this time at Beijing 2008, where he won the Finn class event for a second straight Games.

Unfortunately for Ainslie, rules were changed for the 2013 America's Cup, ruling out the monohulled boat planned by Team Origin and ending its challenge. But by the time a decision had been taken, he had returned already for occasional turns in the Finn, proving that his old skill was there still when he won the first of the 2011 World Cup series regattas in Melbourne.

Should he win a gold medal again at the London 2012 Games, Ainslie would eclipse the achievements of Paul Elvström, the greatest of all Olympic sailors, who won four gold medals at successive Games between 1948 and 1960. 'I guess I am fortunate that I am still very passionate about winning,' he said.

But already there is no other to compare with a man who has been chosen as British Yachtsman of the Year on five occasions and World Sailor of the Year a record three times and has won eight World and European championships.

'For me, his achievement is as valid as (that of Michael) Phelps or (Usain) Bolt,' Jacques Rogge, the International Olympic Committee president, said when presenting Ainslie with his third World Sailor of the Year award. It was a thoroughly deserved accolade.

# IAIN **PERCY**

**Born:** 21 March 1976, Southampton, England
**Height:** 1.85m (6ft)
**Weight:** 95kg (109lb)
**Olympic highlights:**
2000: Finn gold
2004: Star 6th
2008: Star gold

**Iain Percy decided not to defend his Finn class title from Sydney 2000 to give his best friend a shot at winning the same race at Athens 2004. When this plan fell through, the friends just paired up in the Star class at Beijing 2008 and won gold.**

Iain Percy and Andrew Simpson were friends from the age of seven. They sailed together, raced each other and were buddies off the water. When Percy was chosen by Britain to compete at the Sydney 2000 Games, Simpson was his understudy and training partner.

That was in the Finn class, the heaviest Olympic class for single-handed sailors and perfect for heavier, taller men. Percy won the Olympic gold in Sydney, and then chose to step aside to campaign for selection in a different boat, a Star, the oldest

Percy celebrates his gold medal after taking the title in the Finn class at Sydney 2000. He received an MBE for his services to Sailing at the end of the same year.

Olympic class. One reason for this was to give Simpson, the friend he called Bart after the cartoon character, a clear run at selection in a Finn for the Athens 2004 Games.

Unfortunately, it did not work out as they had hoped. Ben Ainslie, the Olympic champion in the Laser class in 2000, had also decided to switch to a Finn for 2004, and he beat Simpson to gain the only place available for selection on the British team. So again Simpson was an Olympic understudy. Percy, meanwhile, had helmed a two-man Star keelboat with Steve Mitchell and finished a disappointing sixth in Athens. 'The worst moment in my career,' Percy called it.

So in 2007, when Mitchell became a coach, Percy invited Simpson to become his crew in the Star. Their first success together came remarkably quickly at the Beijing 2008 Games. The pair was second going into the final day's race, but when they awoke to see the customary quiet waters churned by wind and rain, they knew gold could be theirs.

'When we saw the wind and rain, we knew. We are Brits. We live for that stuff. And anyway we told each other the weather doesn't matter. We had more talent on board than anyone,' said Percy. They had to finish ahead of the Swedish boat to win gold, and they did so in fifth place. 'To do it with my mate of 25 years means everything,' said Percy.

He had sailed first on a family holiday on the Norfolk Broads, but in small dinghies in the Solent, near where his father was a GP. 'The family took up the sport together,' he said. At 16 he won an under-19 National Championship and by 20 he was understudy on the British Olympic team to Ainslie in the Laser at the Atlanta 1996 Games.

He switched to the Finn after seeing Ainslie win the Olympic silver in the Laser to give himself a clearer path to Olympic selection in 2000, and to suit his naturally heavier frame in the larger Finn class. It paid handsomely, because he sailed so well in Sydney that he led into the final race, and the only man who could then deny him gold, Fredrik Loof, had to finish in the first five to do it. Percy out-manoeuvred his opponent, restricting him to 11th and giving himself a comfortable margin of victory.

He chose to switch immediately to the two-man Star class for a fresh challenge instead, so removing himself from competition for the Olympic place with his friend Ainslie, who was moving from the Laser class. Steve Mitchell, almost six years his senior, offered to crew and they were an instant success. In 2002 they became the first British pair to win the World Championship in the Star, and they were to win medals in the next three championships.

But they were never contenders in the light winds off the coast of Athens in 2004. They took third in two races, but the Brazilian boat helmed by Torben Grael won so comfortably that they did it with a day's racing to spare. Percy and Mitchell finished sixth. They came back the following year to win the European Championships together, but that marked the end of their partnership.

Percy and Simpson, however, plan to continue their campaign together for a chance of a gold medal in 2012. Together they won the European title in 2009, and a year later they followed up with victory at the World Championships. This was all the more remarkable because they had spent just 25 days in a Star boat in the previous 12 months, since Percy was committed instead to Britain's potential America's Cup entry, Team Origin. Most remarkable of all was that they came very close to winning the world title with a day to spare.

Team Origin was withdrawn as a challenger at the end of 2010 when the America's Cup rules changed to make a monohull challenge unrealistic, but not before Percy had crewed for Ainslie to win the world match-racing championships, the latest proof that the two men are the most outstanding sailors Britain has ever produced.

Percy moved from the Finn to the two-man Star class and by Beijing 2008 was winning gold in that event too, paired with Andrew Simpson. This was Percy's second gold in two different classes.

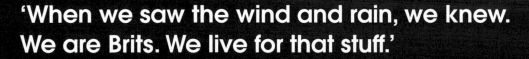

**'When we saw the wind and rain, we knew. We are Brits. We live for that stuff.'**

**Percy,** on the conditions that helped set up his Beijing 2008 gold.

# REBECCA **ADLINGTON**

**Born:** 17 February 1989, Mansfield, England
**Height:** 1.79m (5ft 10in)
**Weight:** 71kg (156lb)
**Olympic highlights:**
2008: 400m Freestyle gold; 800m Freestyle gold

**In 2008, Rebecca Adlington became the first British swimmer to win two gold medals at a single Olympic Games for a century, only three years after serious illness threatened her future in the sport.**

Three years before Rebecca Adlington became the first British woman to win a Swimming gold medal at the Olympic Games for almost half a century, she was struck down by an illness that made training almost impossible.

Adlington was taken ill at the age of 15 with glandular fever, which left her suffering with chronic fatigue syndrome. A sister who suffered the same virus earlier had been forced to give up Swimming. Another was so badly affected that the virus attacked her brain and left her in intensive care.

Adlington had been targeting the 2006 Melbourne Commonwealth Games when it occurred. Instead she was out of the water for weeks and when she returned, could do nothing resembling the training programme of an elite swimmer. 'Every time I got in the water I felt like I couldn't go anywhere. I felt like I weighed 40 stone (255kg),' said Adlington.

Adlington competes in the 400m Freestyle at Beijing 2008. Winning the event gave her the first of her two golds at the Games.

Adlington had learned to swim aged four and joined her local swimming club at the Sherwood Colliery Swimming Baths at seven. Her first competitive swims came two years later and she was eventually invited to train with the county squad. That was where she met Bill Furniss, the coach who was to steer her to the Olympic podium.

She had the physical attributes of height and broad shoulders. But so did others. What made her different was her mental strength and determination to succeed. 'I am the most driven person. I want to make something of my life. I don't want to look back and regret things,' she said in explaining her willingness to continue rising at 5.30 each morning to follow the training programme Furniss laid down.

Furniss, who had coached her since she started training on a daily basis at the age of 13, decided that she needed to keep the mechanics of water training after the virus had passed its worst stage, and continue swimming, but without damaging herself through the quantity of her work. It meant that she had to give up any hope of going to the Melbourne Commonwealth Games, but it helped her return to fitness for the European Championships later that year. She won a silver medal in the 800m Freestyle.

Her real breakthrough came 18 months later with victory at the World Short-Course Championships in Manchester, an hour's drive from her home in Mansfield. As one swimming magazine put it, she 'scared' the 800m world record, missing it by a quarter of a second with a time of 8:8.25, a European and Commonwealth record that surpassed the British record. 'I never expected to go that quick,' she said.

That marked her as a potential Olympic champion in the event. What nobody, even herself, expected when she came to the Beijing 2008 Games was victory in the 400m Freestyle, a distance that was not her forte. Yet she announced herself with a Commonwealth record in the heats and won the final to end Britain's gold famine in women's Swimming that had begun after Anita Lonsbrough won gold at the Rome 1960 Games.

**'I am the most driven person. I want to make something of my life.'**

Adlington celebrates top spot on the podium, finishing Beijing 2008 with golds in the 400m and 800m Freestyle events.

'An unexpected bonus,' Adlington called it. Her parents, who like their daughter believed the 400m was only a warm-up for her, were still travelling to Beijing when she won.

But they sat in the front row for the main event, the 800m, and Adlington did not disappoint. She set a new Olympic record in her heat and won a second gold by a margin of six seconds, smashing the world record by two seconds in a time of 8:14.10.

'It was the most painful race in my whole life. When I finished my body collapsed, probably because I pushed it a bit too far. Afterwards my body hurt,' she said.

The British public took her to its heart, in part because of her simple charm and modesty in victory. 'If we could make a human being capable of curing the world's ills, she wouldn't be a lot unlike Rebecca,' said Furniss. 'She is honest, hard-working and trusting to a fault. You could probably say prim and proper. Just don't get in her way when she's swimming.'

The plaudits and awards that followed a double Olympic triumph left her little time to prepare for the following season's competition. She set a personal best time for the 400m Freestyle at the World Championships but came away with only bronze, and in the 800m Freestyle she finished fourth.

Adlington's return to the forefront of world Swimming came in 2010. In the European Championships she won gold in the 400m Freestyle and a bronze in the 4 x 200m Freestyle Relay. In the 2010 Delhi Commonwealth Games later that year she won both the 400m and 800m Freestyle events, the latter after leading from start to finish. At the year's end she was ranked first in the world at 800m and second at 400m, a perfect launching pad for the defence of her crowns at London in 2012.

# DAVID **WILKIE**

**Born:** 8 March 1954, Colombo, Sri Lanka
**Height:** 1.82m (5ft 11in)
**Weight:** 76kg (167lb)
**Olympic highlights:**
1972: 200m Breaststroke silver
1976: 200m Breaststroke gold; 100m Breaststroke silver

**The most successful British swimmer for 68 years, David Wilkie was the only non-American to win a men's Swimming event at the Montreal 1976 Olympic Games and the first Briton to win a US National Championship.**

David Wilkie was not the most assiduous of trainers in his early swimming career in Scotland, but he had a natural talent that on a modest training programme took him to a silver medal in the 200m Breaststroke at the Munich 1972 Games. Indeed, the American John Hencken needed to break the world record for the event just to beat Wilkie at those Games.

Yet earlier that year his coaches at his Edinburgh club had to talk him out of quitting in a 30-minute showdown in which they persuaded him that it was only worth continuing if he would commit himself to training. 'At the back of my mind there had been a thought that I could be a great swimmer, but I was just too lazy. I had no desire to compete,' said Wilkie.

It was the stiff talking-to that produced the performance that followed in the Olympic Games. 'The decision that I should totally commit myself to the Olympic idea was probably one of the most important in my life – even if it did come late,' said Wilkie.

It convinced the man born to Scottish parents in the Sri Lankan capital of Colombo that he could

**'Watching earlier ceremonies, I thought, "What an emotional moment it must be." And it was. It was great, it really was.'** Wilkie, after winning gold at Montreal 1976.

Wilkie, a Sri Lankan-born Scot who trained in Florida, won the 200m Breaststroke for Britain at the Montreal 1976 Games.

make more of his gifts. He won a sports scholarship to the University of Miami which had excellent facilities, more demanding training and stiffer competition in the pool.

Long-haired, with long sideburns and a moustache, Wilkie's look was sportingly teased by his teammates. But whatever image that portrayed, he became a fighter in the pool and a worker in training.

In 1973 he broke Hencken's world 200m Breaststroke record to win the world title in Belgrade, and a year later he won gold medals in 200m Breaststroke and 200m Individual Medley in both the Commonwealth Games and the European Championships. In the 200m Individual Medley at the latter, he set another world record.

At the World Championships in 1975 Wilkie first won the 100m Breaststroke in a European and Commonwealth record time, and beat those same records in the 200m Breaststroke two days later to win that title too. Only Hencken had ever swum faster, and the American had chosen to miss the World Championships.

The two rivals came into competition again at the NCAA Championships in early 1976. Hencken won the 100yd, Wilkie the 200yd. The following week, at the US Championships, he beat Hencken into second place in the 100m Breaststroke, beat him again in the 200m and completed a hat-trick of victories in the 200m Individual Medley. No Briton had ever won a US Championship before Wilkie, and here he was winning three.

It was the psychological advantage over Hencken he needed going into the Montreal 1976 Olympic Games. But Hencken set world-record times in each round of the 100m there, beating Wilkie into the silver-medal position by 0.32 seconds in the final. Wilkie's own time was a European and Commonwealth record, and well inside the pre-Games world record.

The 100m was Wilkie's secondary event. It was the 200m he wanted to win more. He planned to take it easy in his heat but still broke the Olympic record, and was a full three seconds faster than the next-quickest qualifier. 'I knew then the race was as good as won so long as something didn't go wrong,' he said in his autobiography.

Wilkie's plan was to be behind until the third length, catch up on that and lead only on the final length. Instead, he led at the first turn, so slowed deliberately to let Hencken lead. 'On the third length I moved, and I thought John might come with me but he didn't seem to have anything. I knew that was it, that he couldn't bring it back on the fourth. I stopped even being aware of him, for our contest was over and it just became a race against the clock,' said Wilkie.

The clock was well and truly beaten. Hencken beat his own world record by a second but Wilkie beat him by more than two seconds, and the record by 3.11 seconds. Onlookers regarded it as the performance of the Games in the pool. 'One must ask what sort of swimmer, what kind of man, can break the 200m world record by 3.10 seconds. Just fantastic!' wrote the reporter for *Australian International Swimmer* magazine.

'You think about winning the gold medal but when you actually do you are living it. On the rostrum it was my time, completely mine and nobody else's,' said Wilkie, the only non-American man to win a Swimming gold medal at the Montreal 1976 Olympic Games.

He was chosen as European Swimming's Man of the Year for a third straight year, and his record of three Olympic, five world, two European and four Commonwealth medals, as well as three world, nine European and 19 Commonwealth records, has not been surpassed by any British swimmer.

A moment to treasure for Wilkie as he is presented with his gold medal for the 200m Breaststroke at Montreal 1976.

# CHARLOTTE **COOPER**

**Born:** 22 September 1870, Ealing, England
**Olympic highlights:**
1900: Tennis Singles gold; Tennis Mixed Doubles gold

**Charlotte Cooper was not the first woman to win an Olympic title, but she will forever be the first to have won an individual event at the modern Olympic Games when she competed in Tennis at the Paris 1900 Games.**

Charlotte Cooper was the first woman to win an Olympic title in an individual event, in the Tennis Singles. Her ankle-length dress and black shoes show how important decorum was.

For the best part of a century the annals of the Olympic movement recorded that a British Tennis player, Charlotte Cooper, was the first woman to win an Olympic title. Recent research has shown it was in reality a Swiss sailor, Madame la Comtesse Hélène de Pourtalès, a crew member in her husband's six-metre yacht.

Yet Cooper remains the first to win in an individual sport – not receiving a gold medal, because they were not awarded in 1900 – when she beat the Frenchwoman Hélène Prévost 6-1, 6-4 in the Singles – on the introduction of a women's tournament. She will also forever be the first woman to win a second Olympic title, when she partnered Reginald Doherty to victory in the Mixed Doubles at the same Games.

Cooper was one of several outstanding British female tennis players of her time. Lottie Dod had won five Wimbledon Singles titles before Cooper. Dorothea Chambers was to win seven and an Olympic title in 1908. Yet Cooper's record in the annual Wimbledon tournament, then in its infancy at the All-England Lawn Tennis and Croquet Club in south London, marks her as one of the all-time greats of the game.

Known as 'Chattie', she was tall and slender and something of a sprinter. She trained by running up and down stairs at her home but in the manner of the times, she had to play in an ankle-length dress, which severely limited her athleticism.

She was to win the Wimbledon title on five occasions. After the first in 1895, she cycled back to the Surbiton home of her brother, where she was staying during the tournament. On her return, her brother is supposed to have asked, 'What have you being doing, Chattie?' as he pruned roses in his front garden. 'I've just won the Championship,' she replied. Her brother simply shrugged and said nothing, not realising the significance of what he had just been told, and returned to his pruning.

Her last win at Wimbledon was in 1908, by which time she was 37 years and 282 days old. To this day she remains the oldest winner and also the oldest finalist, because four years later she was to finish as runner-up, at the age of 41.

She also won the Scottish and Welsh Singles titles in the last decade of the 19th century, and she was a regular winner at the Irish Championships too. In all, she amassed a total of eight Irish Championships, including Singles, Doubles and Mixed Doubles in 1895.

Cooper married fellow player and official Alfred Sterry, and she remained involved in tennis throughout her long life. Their daughter, Gwen, played for Britain's Wightman Cup team and their son Rex became vice-chairman of the All-England club. Their grandson Brian played rugby union for Scotland, as had their son-in-law. Mrs Skerry died in 1966 at the age of 96, making her the longest-living British Olympic champion.

# LAUNCESTON **ELLIOT**

**Launceston Elliot was Britain's first Olympic champion, but he was to be better known as a famous music-hall strongman who entertained audiences across Europe with incredible feats of strength.**

**Born:** 9 June 1874, Mumbai, India
**Height:** 1.87m (6ft 1in)
**Weight:** 102kg (224lb)
**Olympic highlights:**
1896: One-handed Lift gold; Two-handed Lift silver

Launceston Elliot was a giant by the standards of his day with a chest measuring 137cm (54in) and biceps 46cm (18.5in). This powerful physique brought him a host of sporting honours before he turned it to his financial advantage in circuses and music halls.

Elliot – the son of a vicar who named him after the Tasmanian town in which he was conceived – was Scottish by ancestry, a kinsman of the Earl of Minto mentioned in *Debrett's Peerage*. He was born in India, where his father was a magistrate, and came to England at the age of 13.

Already massive for his age, he began to be trained in Weightlifting. At the age of 20, he won the British title and decided to attend the Athens 1896 Games, the first modern Olympic Games. He entered whatever event he could. He ran in a round of the 100m in Athletics, and competed at Wrestling and in the Rope Climbing, which was part of the Gymnastics programme.

It was as a weightlifter that the Games annals record him as Britain's first winner. He almost won the Two-handed Lift, achieving the same weight of 111.5kg (245lb) as Viggo Jensen, but the Greek Prince George, who was supervising, gave victory to the Dane on the grounds that he had achieved his weight 'with better style'. In the One-handed Lift, Elliot reversed their positions, winning by 14kg (30lb) with a lift of 71kg (156lb).

He made more impact in the Greek capital because of his good looks. 'This young gentleman attracted universal attention by his uncommon type of beauty,' said the Games' official report. One woman offered her hand in marriage.

He won more British titles and travelled to the Paris 1900 Games, where he competed in the Discus Throw – finishing 11th – when he discovered that Weightlifting was not on the programme. He finally turned professional in 1905, starting with an act with another strongman engaging in mock gladiatorial contests.

Their act, which took them to Paris and Berlin, ended with him showing off his strength by lifting members of the public, and his most famous exhibition of strength: he would support a yoke across his shoulders with a bicycle and rider suspended at each end. The cyclists would pedal at the pace Elliot revolved until centrifugal force launched them into the air in a horizontal position. 'The bikes literally went over the orchestra, who were pounding away on drums,' wrote his daughter years later.

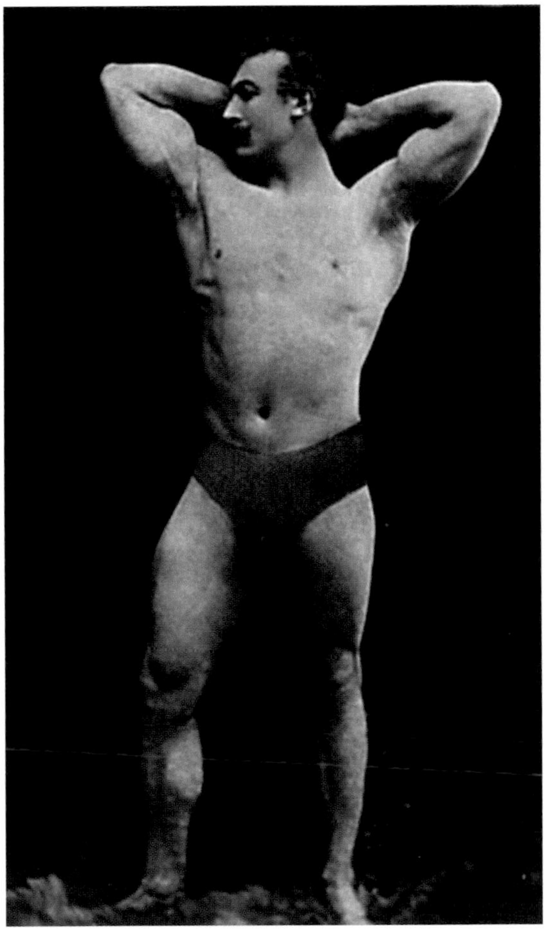

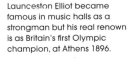

Launceston Elliot became famous in music halls as a strongman but his real renown is as Britain's first Olympic champion, at Athens 1896.

**'This young gentleman attracted universal attention by his uncommon type of beauty.'**

The official report of the Athens 1896 Games.

# The Austerity Olympics 1948

**For a second time in the city's history, in 1948 London hosted an Olympic Games with only two years' notice. For a second time it did so with a tiny budget again and made a small profit. More significantly, it rescued the Olympic Movement.**

The British capital agreed to host the Games of the XIV Olympiad – there was no other city offering – just nine months after the Second World War ended in Europe, costing it one quarter of its national wealth. Severe rationing of food was still imposed, the destruction left by bombing still to be cleared and a severe housing shortage was being solved by tiny pre-fabricated huts.

Yet against all these odds the British put together a record-breaking Games. More nations (59) were present, representative of every continent, more competitors (4099) than ever before and more events than in the previous Games in Berlin 12 years earlier. Television coverage was in homes for the first time – the BBC paid 1000 guineas for the rights – but crowds filled the arenas (668,000 for athletics alone).

A competitor at London 2012 would not recognise the 1948 Games. Many sports, such as Beach Volleyball, Mountain Biking and BMX had not been invented. Athletes were housed not ina purpose-built village, but in military camps, converted school classrooms and college dormitories. Food for competitors was rationed, as it was for the rest of the British public, but athletes were allowed the extra rations permitted to workers in heavy industry. Eggs, fruit and vegetables were donated by other countries; food parcels came from North America and elsewhere in the British Empire.

There was no official transport for athletes. All were given vouchers to travel to their events on the Underground or public buses. Some hitchhiked. None is known to have missed their event.

There were still vestiges of Victorian thinking. It was not considered right that women should compete in Athletics events beyond 200m or the Pole Vault, nor were there Cycling or Equestrian events for them.

Class still pervaded the competition. In one Equestrian event – the Team Dressage – participation was restricted to commissioned officers. When a member of the gold-medal-

John Mark, the President of Cambridge University Athletic Club, was chosen to carry the Olympic Torch at the London 1948 Games opening ceremony.

## 'I'm convinced that if Britain had not been prepared, in spite of barely recovering from the war, to host those 1948 Games, the whole movement might have foundered.'

***Dame Mary Glen Haig**, a fencer in 1948 and later an IOC member, writing in the book,* How London Rescued the Games.

winning Swedish team was found to be only a sergeant, the whole team was disqualified.

But barriers were falling. Women contested Canoeing for the first time. An American, Audrey Patterson, became the first black woman to win an Olympic medal when she took bronze in Athletics; a day later another American, Alice Coachman, became the first black woman to win in the High Jump, edging out Briton Dorothy Tyler – who achieved the same height – because she required only one attempt. There was also the first recorded defection when the Czech president of the Gymnastics technical committee sought political asylum in Britain.

But the nationalism of 1936, which was to return at the Helsinki 1952 Games with the arrival of the Soviet Union team, was absent. It was an austerity Olympics, but also a friendly Games.

Remembered, too, for its great heroes, none greater than one of only 355 women taking part, Dutch housewife Fanny Blankers-Koen, who was already 30 and a mother of two. She had set world records in six different events during the war years but rules permitted her to contest only four Athletics events. She chose the 100m and 200m, the 80m Hurdles and to anchor the Dutch team in the 4 x 100m Relay. She won all four. A grateful Dutch nation later presented her with a bicycle, 'so you don't have to run so much'.

More great athletes appeared. Emil Zátopek, a Czech soldier who was to win three gold medals in 1952, won his first in the 10,000m in London. Bob Mathias, 17, who tried the Decathlon for the first time four months before the Games, won the event, as he was to do four years later in Helsinki. Harrison Dillard, the world-record holder in the 110m Hurdles, was not chosen for the event but won the 100m instead, and returned to the Helsinki 1952 Games to win his speciality event.

Britain entered 313 competitors – it will probably be twice as many in 2012 – but won only three gold medals: two in Rowing and the other in Sailing. The hosts were 12th in the medal table.

But however the performances of the British were judged, there was nothing but praise for the remarkable achievement of pulling off a Games – with little more than two years' notice – that put the Olympic movement back on track after a long absence. 'How could such a project in the Grand Manner be accomplished in the threadbare and impoverished world of 1948?' asked IOC president Sigfrid Edstrom. He called it the 'supreme challenge' – and the result? 'A triumph... an unqualified success,' he wrote.

Above: Opening ceremonies were not lavish by today's standards but were still eagerly watched. Here the Swedish Gymnastic Association's members put on a display at Wembley Stadium for the London 1948 Games.

# The Changing Face of the London Olympic Games

The scale of the Olympic Games has grown dramatically. By 2012, London will have hosted the Games three times, a record for any city. The London 1908 Games were held at the purpose-built White City Stadium (below). Its compact design was able to accommodate Cycling, Athletics and Swimming (the pool can be seen on the right of the picture). By contrast, the centrepiece of the London 2012 Games is the magnificent Olympic Stadium (bottom). Cycling and Swimming now have their own venues.

Above: The London 1908 Games, at the White City stadium in west London.

Below: An artist's impression of the London 2012 Olympic Stadium, in east London.

# Index


4 x 100m Medley
Duncan Goodhew 110
4 x 100m Relay
Allan Wells 52-3
Harold Abrahams 10
Lynn Davies 18-19
Mary Rand 44-5
4 x 200m Freestyle
Henry Taylor 115
Paul Radmilovic 114
4 x 400m Relay
David Hemery 24-7
Lord Burghley 12-13
Sally Gunnell 22-3
50m Rifle, Three Positions
Malcolm Cooper 104-5
100m
Allan Wells 52-3
Harold Abrahams 10
100m Backstroke
Judy Grinham 111
100m Breaststroke
Adrian Moorhouse 113
David Wilkie 116-17
Duncan Goodhew 110
110m Hurdles
Lord Burghley 12-13
200m
Allan Wells 52-3
Harold Abrahams 10
200m Breaststroke
Anita Lonsborough 112
David Wilkie 116-17
400m
Ann Packer 42
Eric Liddell 38
Wyndham Halswelle 54-5
400m Freestyle
Henry Taylor 115
Rebecca Adlington 108-9
400m Hurdles
David Hemery 24-7
Lord Burghley 12-13
Sally Gunnell 22-3
400m Individual Medley
Anita Lonsborough 112
500m Time Trial
Victoria Pendleton 70
800m
Albert Hill 28-9
Ann Packer 42
Douglas Lowe 39
Kelly Holmes 30-3
Sebastian Coe 14-15
Steve Ovett 36-7, 40-1
800m Freestyle
Rebecca Adlington 108-9
800m Hurdles
Mary Rand 44-5
1500m
Albert Hill 28-9
Kelly Holmes 30-3
Sebastian Coe 14-15
Steve Ovett 36-7, 40-1
1500m Freestyle
Henry Taylor 115
3000m Steeplechase
Chris Brasher 11
3000m Team Race
Albert Hill 28-9
1km Time Trial
Chris Hoy 66-9

**A**

Abrahams, Harold 10, 12, 16, 17, 28
Adlington, Rebecca 108-9
Ainslie, Ben 94-7, 99, 100
Akii-Bua, Jon 27
Allan, Alister 105
Allhusen, Derek 78, 80
Amsterdam 1928 Olympics Games
Douglas Lowe 39
Jack Beresford 86-7
Lord Burghley 12-13
Antwerp 1920 Olympics Games
Albert Hill 28-9
Harold Abrahams 10
Harry Mallin 57
Henry Taylor 115
Jack Beresford 86-7
Paul Radmilovic 114
Argenton, Alessandro 81
Arnold, Dave 30
Athens 1896 Olympic Games
Launceston Elliot 119
Athens 2004 Olympic Games
Ben Ainslie 94-7
Bradley Wiggins 74-5
Chris Hoy 66-9
Denise Lewis 34-5
Iain Percy 100-1
Jason Queally 71
Kelly Holmes 30-3
Matthew Pinsent 88-9
Nicole Cooke 64-5
Rebecca Romero 72-3
Sarah Ayton 102-3
Shirley Robertson 102-3
Tim Brabants 60-1
Victoria Pendleton 70
Athletics
Albert Hill 28-9, 39
Allan Wells 52-3
Ann Packer 42
Chris Brasher 11
Daley Thompson 48-51
David Hemery 24-7
Denise Lewis 34-5
Douglas Lowe 39
Eric Liddell 16, 17, 38
Harold Abrahams 10, 12, 16, 17, 28
Jonathan Edwards 20-1
Kelly Holmes 30-3
Lord Burghley 12-13, 17, 26
Lynn Davies 18-19
Mary Peters 43
Mary Rand 44-5
Sally Gunnell 22-3
Sebastian Coe 14-15, 36-7, 40
Steve Ovett 14, 36-7, 40-1
Tessa Sanderson 46-7
Wyndham Halswelle 54-5
Atlanta 1996 Olympic Games
Ben Ainslie 94-7
Chris Boardman 62-3
Denise Lewis 34-5
Jonathan Edwards 20-1
Kelly Holmes 30-3
Matthew Pinsent 88-9
Shirley Robertson 102-3
Steve Redgrave 90-3
Tessa Sanderson 46-7
Ayton, Sarah 102-3

**B**

Badger, Roscoe 55
Baker, Philip 29
Bannister, Roger 11
Barber, Eunice 34, 35
Barcelona 1992 Olympic Games
Adrian Moorhouse 113
Chris Boardman 62-3
Jonathan Edwards 20-1
Matthew Pinsent 88-9
Sally Gunnell 22-3
Sean Kerly 83
Shirley Robertson 102-3
Steve Redgrave 90-3
Tessa Sanderson 46-7
Barclay, Sir Harry 28
Beamon, Bob 18
Beijing 2008 Olympic Games
Ben Ainslie 94-7
Bradley Wiggins 74-5
Chris Hoy 66-9
Iain Percy 100-1
Nicole Cooke 64-5
Rebecca Adlington 108-9
Rebecca Romero 72-3
Sarah Ayton 102-3
Tim Brabants 60-1
Victoria Pendleton 70
Beresford, Jack 86-7
Berlin 1936 Olympic Games
Jack Beresford 86-7
Beyer, Olaf 37
Bigg, Jon 23
Boardman, Chris 62-3, 65, 68, 74
Bos, Thei 69
Boston, Ralph 19
Boxing
Chris Finnegan 56
Harry Mallin 57
Dick McTaggart 58
Terry Spinks 59
Brabants, Tim 60-1
Brailsford, David 69
Brasher, Chris 11
Brightwell, Robbie 42
Brooke-Houghton, Julian 99
Broome, David 81
Brousse, Roger 58
Brugger, Andreas 15
Budgett, Richard 88
Bunn, Darrell 34
Burghley, Lord 12-13, 17, 26
Byers, Tom 40
Bylehn, Erik 39

C
Canoeing
Tim Brabants 60-1
Carpenter, John 54-5
Cavendish, Mark 75
Chariots of Fire 12, 16-17, 38
Charnley, Dave 59
Chataway, Chris 11, 33
Clark, Saskia 103
Coe, Sebastian 14-15, 36-7, 40, 51
Commenee, Charles van 34
Conley, Mike 21
Cook, Stephanie 85
Cooke, Nicole 64-5
Cooper, Charlotte 118
Cooper, Malcolm 104-5
Cracknell, James 91, 93
Cram, Steve 36, 40
Cromwell, Dean B. 27
Cross, Martin 88
Cycling
Bradley Wiggins 74-5
Chris Boardman 62-3
Chris Hoy 66-9
Jason Queally 71
Nicole Cooke 64-5
Rebecca Romero 72-3
Victoria Pendleton 70

D
Davies, Chris 98
Davies, Lynn 18-19, 52
Decathlon
Daley Thompson 48-51
Dempsey, Bob 103
deRiel, Emily 85
Dick, Frank 50
Disley, John 11
Dobrescu, Mircea 57
Domolky, Lidia 82
Double Sculls (2x)
Jack Beresford 86-7

E
Edgar, Ross 69
Edwards, Jonathan 20-1
Eights (8x)
Jack Beresford 86-7
Elliott, John 56
Elliot, Launceston 119
Ellison, Adrian 88
Elstrom, Sigfrid 13
Elvestrom, Paul 97
Equestrian
Derek Allhusen 78
Harry Llewellyn 79
Richard Meade 80-1
Europe
Shirley Robertson 102-3

F
Farmer-Patrick, Sandra 23
Fencing
Gillian Sheen 82
Finn
Ben Ainslie 94-7
Iain Percy 100-1
Finnegan, Chris 56
Flintoff-King, Debbie 23
Flood, Debby 73
Florent, Guillaume 97
Floyd, Stanley 53
Fly Weight
Terry Spinks 59
Flying Dutchman
Rodney Pattisson 98-9
Foil
Gillian Sheen 82
Football 106-7
Forse, Jack 56
Foster, Bob 56
Foster, Tim 91, 92, 93
Fours (4-)
Jack Beresford 86-7
Matthew Pinsent 88-9
Steve Redgrave 90-3
Fours (4+)
Steve Redgrave 90-3
Fox, Jim 85
Freemsan, Cathy 21
Fry, C.B. 21

G
Garrett-Gilmore, William 86
Glen-Haig, Mary 82
Gold, Sir Arthur 24
Goodhew, Duncan 110
Gordon-Watson, Mary 80, 81
Grael, Torben 100-1
Grebenyuk, Alekandr 48
Grinham, Judy 111
Grobler, Jurgen 89, 91, 92, 93
Gunn, Dick 56
Gunnell, Sally 22-2
Guyon, Jean-Jacques 78

H
Halswelle, Wyndham 54-5
Harris, Reg 69
Harrison, Kenny 21
Hayes, John 77
Helsinki 1952 Olympics Games
Chris Brasher 11
Gillian Sheen 82
Harry Llewellyn 79
Hemery, David 24-7
Hennige, Gerhard 26
Heptathlon
Denise Lewis 34-5
Hill, Albert 28-9, 39
Hingsen, Jurgen 50-1
Hockey
Sean Kerly 83
Holmes, Andy 88, 89, 92
Holmes, Kelly 30-3
Houghton, Frances 73
Housden, Fred 24
Hoy, Chris 66-9
Hunt, Dan 73

I
Individual Eventing
Derek Allhusen 78
Individual Jumping
Harry Llewellyn 79
Individual Pursuit
Bradley Wiggins 74-5
Chris Boardman 62-3
Rebecca Romero 72-3

J
Javelin
Tessa Sanderson 46-7
Jenner, Bruce 48, 50
Jennings, Margot 32
Johnson, Ben 53
Johnson, Boris 33
Jones, Al 56
Jones, Ben 78

K
Kaidel, Willy 86-7
Keen, Peter 62, 63
Keirin
Chris Hoy 66-9
Kelly, Jack 86
Kelly, Shane 68
Kenny, Jason 69
Kerly, Sean 83
Kilo
Jason Queally 71
Kiselov, Alexei 56
Klammer, Franz 91
Koeverden, Adam van 61
Kratschmer, Guido 50
Krause, Roswitha 73
Kurschat, Harry 59

L
Lagetko, Anatoli 59
Larsen, Erik 61
Larsen, Ernest 11
Laser
Ben Ainslie 94-7
Ledovskaya, Tatyana 23
Lehmann, Jens 63
Leonard, Silvio 52
Lewis, Denise 34-5
Libeer, Rene 57
Liddell, Eric 16, 17, 38
Light Weight
Dick McTaggart 58
Lillak, Tina 47
Llewellyn, Harry 79
London, Jack 29
London 1908 Olympic Games 76-7
Henry Taylor 115
Paul Radmilovic 114
Wyndham Halswelle 54-5
London 1948 Olympic Games 120-1
Harry Llewellyn 79
Long Jump
Lynn Davies 18-19
Mary Rand 44-5
Longden, Bruce 23, 50
Lonsborough, Anita 112
Loof, Frederik 100
Los Angeles 1932 Olympic Games

Jack Beresford 86-7
Lord Burghley 12-13
Los Angeles 1984 Olympic Games
Adrian Moorhouse 113
Allan Wells 52-3
Daley Thompson 48-51
Malcolm Cooper 104-5
Sean Kerly 83
Sebastian Coe 14-15, 37
Steve Ovett 37, 40-1
Steve Redgrave 90-3
Tessa Sanderson 46-7
Lowe, Douglas 39

**M**
MacDonald-Smith, Iain 98
Madison
Bradley Wiggins 74-5
Magne, Frederic 70
Mallin, Harry 57
Manoliu, Lia 47
Martin, Paul 39
Mathias, Bob 48, 51
Matthjisse, Margriet 102
McFarlane, Mike 53
McLean, Craig 70
McNab, Tom 16
McShane, Buster 43
McTaggart, Dick 58
Meade, Richard 78, 80-1
Meares, Anna 70
Melbourne 1956 Olympic Games
Chris Brasher 11
Dick McTaggart 58
Gillian Sheen 82
Judy Grinham 111
Terry Spinks 59
Mennea, Pietro 53
Merckx, Eddie 63
Mexico City 1968 Olympic Games
Chris Finnegan 56
David Hemery 24-7
Derek Allhusen 78
Jim Fox 85
Lynn Davies 18-19
Mary Peters 43
Richard Meade 80-1
Rodney Pattisson 98-9
Middle Weight
Chris Finnegan 56
Harry Mallin 57
Miles-Clark, Jearl 32
Mitchell, Steve 100-1
Modern Pentathlon
Jim Fox 85
Stephanie Cook 84
Montreal 1976 Olympic Games
Daley Thompson 48-51
David Wilkie 116-17
Duncan Goodhew 110
Jim Fox 85
Malcolm Cooper 104-5
Richard Meade 80-1
Rodney Pattisson 98-9
Steve Ovett 40
Tessa Sanderson 46-7
Moorhouse, Adrian 113
Mortimore, Bob 48
Moscow 1980 Olympic Games
Allan Wells 52-3
Daley Thompson 48-51
Duncan Goodhew 110
Sebastian Coe 14-15, 37
Steve Ovett 37, 40-1
Tessa Sanderson 46-7
Mowbray, Alison 73
Munich 1972 Olympic Games
David Hemery 24-7
David Wilkie 116-17
Jim Fox 85
Lynn Davies 18-19
Malcolm Cooper 104-5
Mary Peters 43
Richard Meade 80-1
Rodney Pattisson 98-9
Mussabini, Sam 10, 16, 28
Mutola, Maria 32

**N**
Nightingale, Danny 84
Nimkel, Stefan 68
Nipkow, Daniel 104
Northcliffe, Lord 76

**O**
Obree, Graeme 63
Onischenko, Boris 84
Orban, Olga 82
Ovett, Steve 14, 36-7, 40-1

**P**
Packer, Ann 42
Pairs (2-)
Matthew Pinsent 88-9
Steve Redgrave 90-3
Pairs (2+)
Steve Redgrave 90-3
Paris 1900 Olympic Games
Charlotte Cooper 118
Paris 1924 Olympic Games
Douglas Lowe 39
Eric Liddell 38
Harold Abrahams 10
Harry Mallin 57
Jack Beresford 86-7
Lord Burghley 12-13
Parker, Adrian 84
Parker, Bridget 81
Pattisson, John 98
Pattisson, Rodney 97, 98-9
Pazdzior, Kazimierz 59
Peltzer, Otto 39
Pendleton, Victoria 67, 70
Pentathlon
Derek Allhusen 78
Jim Fox 85
Mary Peters 43
Mary Rand 44-5
Stephanie Cook 84
Percy, Iain 100-1
Peters, Mary 43, 47
Peters, Steve 70
Phelps, Eric 86, 87
Philips, Mark 81
Pickering, Ron 18
Pietri, Dorando 77
Pinsent, Matthew 73, 88-9, 93
Pirsch, Joachim 86-7
Porritt, Arthur 17
Press, Irina 45
Prokhorova, Yelena 35
Prud'homme, Georges 58
Puttnam, David 16

**Q**
Quadruple Sculls
Rebecca Romero 72-3
Quarrie, Don 52
Queally, Jason 68, 71, 74

**R**
Radmilovic, Paul 114
Railey, Zach 97
Rand, Mary 44-5, 74
Rand, Sydney 44
Redgrave, Steve 87, 88-91, 92, 93
Road Race
Nicole Cooke 64-5
Robbins, William 54-5
Robertson, Shirley 102-3
Rome 1960 Olympic Games
Anita Lonsborough 112
Dick McTaggart 58
Gillian Sheen 82
Mary Rand 44-5
Romero, Rebecca 72-3
Rosendahl, Heide 43
Roulston, Hayden 75
Rowing
Jack Beresford 86-7
Matthew Pinsent 88-9
Rebecca Romero 72-3
Steve Redgrave 90-3
Roy, Jack 57
Rozsnyói, Sándor 11
Rudd, Bevil 28, 29

**S**
Sailing
Ben Ainslie 94-7
Iain Percy 100-1
Rodney Pattisson 98-9
Sarah Ayton 102-3
Shirley Robertson 102-3
Samaranch, Juan Antonio 15
Sanderson, Tessa 46-7
Scheidt, Robert 94, 96-7
Scholz, Jackson 17
Schubert, Rainer 26
Scott, Steve 36
Seoul 1988 Olympic Games
Adrian Moorhouse 113
Daley Thompson 48-51
Jonathan Edwards 20-1
Malcolm Cooper 104-5
Sally Gunnell 22-3
Sean Kerly 83

Sebastian Coe 14-15
Steve Redgrave 90-3
Tessa Sanderson 46-7
Sheen, Gillian 82
Sherwood, John 26
Shields, Larry 29
Shirley, Eric 11
Shooting
Malcolm Cooper 104-5
Simpson, Andrew 100, 101
Single Sculls (1x)
Jack Beresford 86-7
Sireau, Kevin 69
Smith, Billy 24, 26
Smith, Francis 88
Snell, Peter 37
South, Ian 72
Southwood, Dick 86, 87
Spinks, Terry 59
Sprint
Chris Hoy 66-9
Victoria Pendleton 70
Stallard, Hyla 'Henry' 39
Star
Iain Percy 100-1
Stewart, Douglas 79
Stockholm 1912 Olympic Games
Henry Taylor 115
Paul Radmilovic 114
Straub, Jurgen 37
Sweeney, Patrick 89
Swimming
Adrian Moorhouse 113
Anita Lonsborough 112
David Wilkie 116-17
Duncan Goodhew 110
Henry Taylor 115
Judy Grinham 111
Paul Radmilovic 114
Rebecca Adlington 108-9
Sydney 2000 Olympic Games
Ben Ainslie 94-7
Bradley Wiggins 74-5
Chris Boardman 62-3
Chris Hoy 66-9
Denise Lewis 34-5
Iain Percy 100-1
Jason Queally 71
Jonathan Edwards 20-1
Kelly Holmes 30-3
Matthew Pinsent 88-9
Shirley Robertson 102-3
Stephanie Cook 84
Steve Redgrave 90-3
Tim Brabants 60-1

**T**

Taylor, Henry 77, 115
Taylor, John 54-5
Taylor, Morgan 12, 13
Team Eventing
Derek Allhusen 78
Team Jumping
Harry Llewellyn 79
Team Pursuit
Bradley Wiggins 74-5
Chris Boardman 62-3
Rebecca Romero 72-3
Team Sprint
Chris Hoy 66-9
Jason Queally 71
Tennis
Charlotte Cooper 118
Time Trial
Chris Boardman 62-3
Nicole Cooke 64-5
Ter-Ovanesyan, Igor 18
Thompson, Daley 48-51
Three-day Eventing
Derek Allhusen 78
Richard Meade 80-1
Tokyo 1964 Olympic Games
Anita Lonsborough 112
Ann Packer 42
Dick McTaggart 58
Jim Fox 85
Lynn Davies 18-19
Mary Peters 43
Mary Rand 44-5
Richard Meade 80-1
Toomey, Bill 45
Tournant, Arnaud 68-9, 71
Triple Jump
Jonathan Edwards 20-1
Trujillo, Rafael 97
Tyler, Dorothy 47

**V**

Vanderstock, Geoff 24, 26
Vos, Marianne 65

**W**

Walker, John 40
Wallace, Ken 61
Water Polo
Paul Radmilovic 114
Webb, Sarah 102, 103
Weightlifting
Launceston Elliot 119
Welland, Colin 16, 17, 38
Wells, Allan 52-3
Wells, Margot 52
West, Debbie 81
Whitbread, Fatima 46-7
White, Densign 47
White, Wilf 79
Wiggins, Bradley 74-5
Wilkie, David 116-17
Wilson, Pippa 103
Wooderson, Sydney 29

**Y**

Yevdokimova, Natalya 32-3
Yngling
Sarah Ayton 102-3
Shirley Robertson 102-3
York, Lisa 30
Young, Wilson 52

# Picture Credits

The publishers would like to thank the following sources for their kind permission to reproduce the pictures in this book.

**Action Images:** /David Gray/Reuters: 109; /Jason Reed/Reuters: 108; /Reuters: 89; /Sporting Pictures UK: 41

**Getty Images:** 50; /Lutz Bongarts/Bongarts: 20; /Clive Brunskill: 32; /Simon Bruty: 90, 91; /David Cannon: 62, 63; /Central Press: 56; /Mark Dadswell: 94; /Carl de Souza/AFP: 68, 69; /Tony Duffy: 34, 36, 37, 43, 49, 113; /Al Fenn/Time & Life Pictures: 42; /Fox Photos/Hulton Archive: 87; /Paul Gilham: 7; /Hulton Archive: 19, 44, 54, 77; /IOC Olympic Museum: 17, 39; /Nick Laham: 74; /Andy Lyons: 35; /Clive Mason: 96, 97; /Jamie McDonald: 65; /Douglas Miller: 26; /Gray Mortimore: 105; /Popperfoto: 11, 21, 24, 27, 45, 79, 82, 86; /Mike Powell: 71; /Steve Powell: 99; /Rolls Press/ Popperfoto: 25; /Pascal Rondeau: 30; /Cameron Spencer: 66, 75; /Michael Steele: 31; / William Sumits/Time & Life Pictures: 121; /Bob Thomas: 15, 22, 52, 53, 83, 85, 104; /Bob Thomas/ Popperfoto: 55, 107; /Topical Press Agency: 76, 118; /Nick Wilson: 92; /Greg Wood/AFP: 67

**ODA:** 122-123B

**Press Association Images:** 16, 38, 59, 78, 81, 93, 98, 111, 112, 114; /AP: 120; /Jon Buckle: 84; /DPA: 51; /Kevork Djansezian/AP: 61; /Empics Sport: 12-13, 28, 57; /Christophe Ena/AP: 64; /Matthew Fearn: 103; /Dawa Gaesang/Landov: 70; /John Giles: 72, 73; /Toby Melville: 100; /Don Morley: 58; /Rebecca Naden: 88; /Phil Noble: 33; /Steve Parsons: 9; /S&G and Barratts: 14, 46, 47, 48, 106, 110, 115, 116, 117, 122-123T; /Neal Simpson: 60, 95, 102; /Topham Picturepoint: 10, 29, 80; /Song Wang/Landov: 101

**Private Collection:** 119

Every effort has been made to acknowledge correctly and contact the source and/or copyright holder of each picture and Carlton Books Limited apologises for any unintentional errors or omissions, which will be, corrected in future editions of this book.